Tapping the Power of

PERSONALIZED LEARNING

ASCD MEMBER BOOK

Many ASCD members received this book as a
member benefit upon its initial release.

Learn more at: **www.ascd.org/memberbooks**

Tapping the Power of

PERSONALIZED LEARNING

A Roadmap for School Leaders

JAMES
RICKABAUGH

 Alexandria, Virginia

1703 N. Beauregard St. • Alexandria, VA 22311-1714 USA
Phone: 800-933-2723 or 703-578-9600 • Fax: 703-575-5400
Website: www.ascd.org • E-mail: member@ascd.org
Author guidelines: www.ascd.org/write

Deborah S. Delisle, *Executive Director;* Stefani Roth, *Publisher;* Genny Ostertag, *Director, Content Acquisitions;* Julie Houtz, *Director, Book Editing & Production;* Ernesto Yermoli, *Editor;* Thomas Lytle, *Senior Graphic Designer;* Mike Kalyan, *Manager, Production Services;* Andrea Wilson, *Senior Production Design Specialist;* Cynthia Stock, *Typesetter*

PAPERBACK ISBN: 978-1-4166-2157-7 ASCD product #116016
PDF E-BOOK ISBN: 978-1-4166-2159-1; see Books in Print for other formats.
Quantity discounts: 10–49, 10%; 50+, 15%; 1,000+, special discounts (e-mail programteam@ascd.org or call 800-933-2723, ext. 5773, or 703-575-5773). For desk copies, go to www.ascd.org/deskcopy.

ASCD Member Book No. FY16-5 (Feb. 2016 P). ASCD Member Books mail to Premium (P), Select (S), and Institutional Plus (I+) members on this schedule: Jan, PSI+; Feb, P; Apr, PSI+; May, P; Jul, PSI+; Aug, P; Sep, PSI+; Nov, PSI+; Dec, P. For current details on membership, see www.ascd.org/membership.

Library of Congress Cataloging-in-Publication Data

Names: Rickabaugh, James.
Title: Tapping the power of personalized learning : a roadmap for school
    leaders / James Rickabaugh.
Description: Alexandria, Virginia : ASCD, 2016. | Includes bibliographical
    references and index.
Identifiers: LCCN 2015042275 | ISBN 9781416621577 (pbk.)
Subjects: LCSH: Individualized instruction.
Classification: LCC LB1031 .R53 2016 | DDC 371.39/4–dc23 LC record available at
    http://lccn.loc.gov/2015042275

23 22 21 20 19 18 17 16   1 2 3 4 5 6 7 8 9 10 11 12

Tapping the Power of

PERSONALIZED LEARNING

A Roadmap for School Leaders

Preface

For 40 years, I have worked in the field of education as a classroom teacher, building and district administrator, author, and consultant. In rural, suburban, and urban school districts, I have seen how our traditional system of education works well for some students and not at all for others.

My experience as an educator has been a journey toward the work I am doing today. Over the years, I have wondered and worried as I've watched some students simply go through the motions of education, never gaining a sense of purpose or discovering a passion in the process, while others seem to flourish through relationships with committed mentors or commitments to causes or content that resonate with them. Why can't all students become engaged and create meaningful connections in school? And, why can't learning in school hold the same attraction that learning outside of it does for so many students?

For the past five years, I've had the privilege of leading a network of educators, schools, and students on a journey to find answers to these vexing questions. What I have to share in this book is the result of that journey: the cumulative work of hundreds of educators and experiences of thousands of students.

In the pages that follow, I use the first-person plural because the lessons I'm sharing represent far more than my own voice and experience. I am honored and humbled to be sharing on behalf of the brave, talented, creative, and committed educators and learners who began this journey when there was no trail to follow.

Here is our story.

Late in the first decade of the new millennium, we as educational leaders in Southeastern Wisconsin were becoming increasingly frustrated. We were facing what should have been good times: every year, the school districts we served received more money than the year before (a trend stretching back as far as anyone could recall). We were blessed with committed, well-prepared educators who really cared about student learning. Our communities were generally supportive of our work—many families moved to the area to send their children to one of our school districts.

Despite all of this, it was becoming increasingly clear to us that what we had done in the past really was not preparing our students for their futures. We also realized that despite increases in funding each year, we were not keeping up with the operating costs of the educational system we had inherited. Each year, rather than allocate additional funds to enhance and expand services and programs, we found ourselves looking for services and programs to cut in order to balance our budgets. Further, we saw educators working harder each year than the year before, facing more and more pressure to be accountable for the success of every learner, yet still not being able to reach too many students—and both the number and variety of such students were growing.

We reached an unavoidable conclusion: there had to be a better way. In response, Tim Gavigan, the forward-looking executive director of our regional educational service agency, took the lead in convening a group of superintendents to engage in a year-long examination, reflection, and learning effort aimed at identifying a more effective course. We formed book studies, arranged to hear from thought leaders, examined our own experiences, and consulted practitioners in other fields who had dealt with the disruptions of major organizational transformation. Ultimately, we concluded that our best bet would be to redesign the way our schools and districts operated, starting at the crucial nexus of learning and teaching.

The result: a commitment to place the learner at the center, personalize learning, and rethink instruction as something we do *with* rather than *to* learners. Dr. Gavigan's leadership and the commitment of the group led us to capture our thinking and vision in the form of a white paper to guide our initial work (CESA #1, 2010). This call to action led to funding from the Cooperative Educational Service Agency (CESA) #1 Board of Control to establish the Institute for Personalized Learning (IPL) to lead the work, develop an action network, provide research and support, and develop a working model for personalized learning. Since Tim Gavigan's retirement, we have been fortunate to have the support of his successor, Mary Gavigan, and the CESA #1 Board of Control to expand the work throughout Southeastern Wisconsin and beyond. Since 2010, I have had the honor of serving as director of the institute and the extreme pleasure of working with some of the most creative, courageous, and committed staff and educators I have ever encountered.

From the beginning, the institute recognized that any acceptable design for personalized learning had to meet at least four criteria. The design would need to

1. Have the capacity to create a clear path to success for each learner.
2. Be sustainable, without significant increases in staff or work required.

3. Be affordable with current resources. (We did not anticipate significant increases in funding going forward, and we
were correct.)
4. Be scalable, so that the approach might eventually include
entire schools and districts.

Five years later, we have much to celebrate about our personalized learning model. Students are experiencing learning
growth that far exceeds projections. Just a few examples:

- In the West Allis–West Milwaukee School district, schools
that have adopted the model have scored 30 percent higher
than the district average on the Northwest Evaluation Association's Measures of Academic Progress with matched
student demographics (Northwest Evaluation Association,
2014). Additionally, a recent analysis by Hanover Research
shows that students who are experiencing this approach
perform significantly better on standardized assessments,
and that the longer students experience the model, the
greater their improvement (Hanover Research, 2015).
- Students at Asa Clark Middle School in Pewaukee, which
has adopted the model schoolwide, are showing two to five
times as much growth on ACT Aspire assessments as the
national average (Pewaukee School District, 2015).
- In the year before implementing the model, more than 100
students did not graduate on time at Reagan High School in
Milwaukee. Three years later, that number is down to fewer
than 5 (Roemer, 2015).
- Student behavior at Walker Elementary School in the
West Allis–West Milwaukee School District has improved
dramatically since the model was implemented. Referrals
to the principal have gone from 30 in the semester prior
to adopting the model to at most 1 per month ever since
(Fischer-Tubbs, 2015).

We see students of all demographic and academic backgrounds benefiting from personalization. Currently, we have projects under way in urban, suburban, and rural communities; affluent and economically challenged neighborhoods; and schools at every level of past performance (with those average or below showing the greatest improvements). Most of the schools implementing the model don't have access to outside grants or special allocations of funds, so they use existing resources.

From an initial dozen, the number of districts involved in our Personalized Learning Network has grown to more than three times as many. The network's geographic reach has also grown from Southeastern Wisconsin to include educators across Wisconsin, Illinois, and Minnesota. This book is about what we have learned on our journey so far, why it matters, the difference it has made for learners and educators, and the potential it holds for the future of formal learning systems.

We have chosen to primarily address principals in this book due to the crucial role that they play in the culture, organization, and operation of schools. They also represent a key link between schools and the larger system. Changes in thinking among principals can have strong ripple effects across an entire school district. We appreciate the often unrecognized contributions of principals and seek to do all that we can to help them find success. To us, they hold the potential to be the greatest champions of personalized learning.

Introduction:
Imagine Schools Where . . .

As you open the door to the elementary classroom and step inside, you are struck by the amount of activity and engagement you see and hear. Students are spread throughout the room. Some are huddled together working on a complex math problem. Two students are reading together. Several are sitting quietly on their own—some reading books, others engrossed in their electronic tablets. A small group of students is talking with the teacher about the next math skill they'll be learning and how they'll be able to use it to solve problems both in and out of the classroom. Still others are practicing new skills—some using pencil and paper, others on personal computers.

You approach a few of the learners and ask them what they're doing. One of them reports that he's about to finish his learning plan to add double-digit numbers with fluency and is scheduled to take an assessment the next day. Another describes her current learning goal to master partial product division; when she reaches her goal, she will demonstrate the process for the rest of the class. Still another student explains that her goal is to learn how math might be applied to gymnastics, her current passion. So far, she has found a variety of applications, from tracking practice repetitions to plotting her floor routine on a mat. She says that she knows there are more complicated math connections that she might study later, and discovering these connections helps her to both understand and enjoy math more.

You wait until the teacher has finished her conversation with the small group and approach her. She explains that these students are all ready to learn a common skill, so she grouped them for strategic instruction—a short, focused form of direct instruction.

Your next stop is a nearby middle school. As you enter a classroom, you again see learners highly engaged in a variety of activities. You notice a few of them at low carrels in one corner of the room working by themselves, a small group that appears to be working on a joint project, some students in pairs, and others cycling through individual conferences with the teacher.

During a break between student conferences, the teacher explains that today his learners are meeting with him to update their goals and, in some cases, to set new goals for the next phase of their work. He notes that managing classroom behavior is almost a thing of the past; he spends much more time now managing learning processes instead. You ask about the key difference between the new model and the old way of doing things. The teacher smiles and explains that he used to spend his time planning, delivering, and following up on lessons and reminding learners to do what he expected of them. Now, he says, they play an active role in setting individual learning goals aligned to standards, planning what and how they will learn, identifying the resources they will need, and determining how to demonstrate their learning. As a result, learners feel a much greater sense of ownership and responsibility for their learning. The teacher works primarily as a coach and adviser, identifying resources and providing specific strategic instruction when necessary, but spends very little time disciplining students for off-task behaviors.

A high school classroom is next on your agenda. Your first impression is that it's much like the elementary and middle school classrooms, but here you see even more independence in learning activities. You learn that some students are out in the community collecting data and meeting with local businesspeople and government officials to gather information for later analysis. Students within the classroom appear to be organizing themselves according to the work they're doing. Some are deeply engaged with work on their computers; others are engaged in virtual conversations with fellow learners from other countries. You learn that this afternoon two students will be presenting their global issues projects to an audience of peers, a professor from the university, and three research scientists from a local biomedical company.

Your conversation with this teacher includes much of what you heard earlier, and you are struck by the extent to which students are planning and guiding their own learning. The teacher notes that learners are using standards to guide their work and measure their performance. Though she's actively involved, she's mostly in a support or even co-learning role rather than that of a traditional instructor.

Following your visit, you stop by a local coffee shop with WiFi access and check achievement data for the three schools you visited. You were not sure what to expect since there did not appear to be a major focus on traditional teaching or preparing for standardized testing. The emphasis seemed to be much more on broader and deeper learning and far less on memorization and rote practice that might be closer to what would be on these tests. To your amazement, the performance of students was very strong; among the highest in the region. You look back to see historical trends and note that five years ago, these schools performed at the average in the region and in some cases below. Over the past few years, their progress has been significant, especially when you reflect on the economic challenges of the communities they serve and diversity of learners in their classes.

What you have just experienced may feel like fiction, but it's not—thanks to the work of the Institute for Personalized Learning (IPL) and its member school districts, it is increasingly a reality across the Midwest, and hopefully soon across the country. The IPL approach to learning and teaching taps the commitment, imagination, and creativity of students and encourages them to serve as active partners in their learning. It focuses on building learning capacity rather than simply accumulating academic content that could be easily accessed online.

This book is about transforming the learning ecosystem we have inherited from our parents and grandparents to better prepare learners for their futures. The world has changed and continues to change dramatically—we can't afford to prepare todays learners for yesterday's challenges or even for today's. Over the past five years, our colleagues in the network and we at the Institute for Personalized Learning have learned a lot about what works in schools and what doesn't. We understand and appreciate the crucial role that education leaders play in determining whether to consider, implement, and sustain transformational change; our purpose is to help you maximize the likelihood of success.

The really good news is that the IPL model draws from the best research on deep and purposeful learning. This is not an approach that relies on "experimenting" with students; rather, it rests on what we have known about real, quality learning since before the creation of schools as we know them today.

In the coming chapters, we will describe the elements of conventional instruction that fall short or even get in the way of student learning and share strategies, practices, and tools to help you redesign your approach. Our goal is to make the model understandable, accessible, and usable regardless of existing conditions at your school. However, for the model to succeed, you must be willing to shift away from what doesn't work and open to trying something new.

A Definition of Personalized Learning

The philosophical shift that occurs when personalized learning transforms practices in a building affects everyone, including me as a school leader. Our roles become less focused on reactive ways to address concerns, whether academic or social-emotional. Instead, our efforts become more global and systemic—we are able to proactively support all students as they grow by investing our time and energies into systems that ensure they have the mindsets and behaviors to be successful in their current and future endeavors.

—Randy Daul, principal, Asa Clark Middle School, Pewaukee, Wisconsin

You've probably heard the term "personalized learning" many times and discovered it to mean many different things. Currently, the best-known and most widely publicized definition is the one included in the U.S. Department of Education's (USDOE) National Education Technology Plan (2010):

> Personalization refers to instruction that is paced to learning needs, tailored to learning preferences, and tailored to the specific interests of different learners. In an environment that is fully personalized, the learning objectives and content as well as the method and pace may all vary (so personalization encompasses differentiation and individualization).

Though helpful, this definition misses a key element of truly personalized learning environments: repositioning of the student within the learning and teaching process. The USDOE definition stops short of recognizing the powerful role students must be allowed to play in setting learning goals, planning their learning paths, tracking their progress, and demonstrating their learning as partners and codesigners alongside educators. It misses the shift in instruction from something we do *to* learners to something we do *with* them, which accounts for the real power of personalization. In a truly personalized environment, learners play a key role in planning, developing, demonstrating, and applying their learning, and in so doing develop greater self-efficacy, ownership, and learning independence—key preparation skills for the lives they will lead and careers they will build.

According to the USDOE definition of personalized learning, each learner pursues unique learning objectives and engages with individually tailored content at a pace that is personally comfortable. One might conclude that such learners may not develop a common body of knowledge or skills and, as a result, that educators are left without a comprehensive view of what learners need to know and be able to do before graduating. An absence of standards debated and adopted by the community risks depriving schools both of a common focus and of accountability to the community and could leave students ultimately unprepared for future success. Without question, learners need to move at their own pace and engage in classroom activities suited to their individual interests and levels of readiness, but alignment of instruction to appropriate standards remains enormously important.

We define truly effective personalized learning as follows:

> An approach to learning and instruction that is designed around individual learner readiness, strengths, needs, and interests. Learners are active participants in setting goals, planning learning paths, tracking progress, and determining how learning will be demonstrated. At any given time, learning objectives, content, methods, and pacing are likely to vary from learner to learner as they pursue proficiency aligned to established standards. A fully personalized environment moves beyond both differentiation and individualization.

Our definition diverges from the traditional approach to instruction in the following ways:

It shifts the roles of learners and educators. Students and teachers move from a model in which teachers make all significant decisions and students are expected to comply, to one where both parties work together to make decisions about learning aligned to standards and intended learning outcomes.

It ensures purposeful learning. Educators and learners actively consider the "why" of learning, and in doing so give meaning and focus to instruction.

It supports individual learning goals and action plans. Personalized learning goes beyond placing learners at the center to actively involving them in designing the learning path, identifying learning options and resources, monitoring progress, and demonstrating what they have learned.

It varies the pace of learning while remaining focused on established standards. Variations in how and how quickly students learn are respected and accommodated to ensure that learning, rather than instruction or curriculum, is the focus.

It focuses on broader concepts and deeper learning. Instruction that prepares students for their futures goes beyond asking students to memorize, organize, and sequence content to engaging students deeply in content and enlisting them to frame problems, design solutions, create models, and build lifelong interests and skills.

It develops collaboration skills and strategies. Personalization does not mean that students are isolated as they learn. To the contrary, working in pairs, in small groups, and as a whole class helps students to develop important social and work skills as they draw from other learners to design, solve problems, and build new knowledge together.

It uses technology as a support. Technology plays a key role in personalized learning, particularly as we work to scale the approach across groups and learning contexts. However, it is limited to a supporting role as a tool to explore, create, collect, analyze, and track data.

It affords learners greater ownership of and influence over learning. When students become more active partners in their learning, their level of commitment and persistence grows as they increasingly feel a vested interest in learning outcomes. They develop the skills necessary to make decisions about and engage independently in their learning long after leaving the classroom.

It supports a variety of learning approaches. By placing learning rather than instruction at its center, the IPL model encourages collaboration between students and teachers in designing a learning path and thus rejects the "one-size-fits-all" approach that most of us experienced as students and too often continue to encounter as educators.

It builds learners' skills and capacity with the support of important content. As noted earlier, personalized learning goes beyond the accumulation of academic content. Although content is very important, its role is to support the skill development and capacity building necessary for continued learning.

It fosters learning independence. Our ultimate goal is for students to no longer have to depend on us for their learning. Our purpose as educators is to support them as they become increasingly independent, accrue skills, and make choices in pursuit of meeting established standards.

Technology and Personalized Learning

Advertisements presenting the benefits of technology in education might lead you to conclude that the more technology students have at their disposal, the more personalized their learning is. If this were true, you'd expect personalized learning to be well under way throughout the United States, given the amount of money we spend on technology in schools. Unfortunately, there is little evidence that investing more in technology has "moved the needle" at all in terms of academic achievement (Tamim, Bernard, Barokhovski, Abrami, & Schmid, 2011). Certainly, data on the effect of technology on academic achievement do not suggest that more technology alone will lead to better outcomes for students. One of the problems is that educators too often employ technology to support conventional learning activities that have been around for generations—think worksheets and print reading. What's more, educators often fear that technology strips them of control over instruction and leaves them unable to adequately assess student progress—a justifiable concern at a time when educators are confronted with demands to keep up with technology while simultaneously relying on assessment measures from bygone eras.

Nevertheless, technology plays an important role in personalized learning. One of the best descriptions of its role that we have encountered is from Mary Ann Wolf:

> Personalized learning requires not only a shift in the design of schooling, but also a leveraging of modern technologies. Personalization cannot take place at scale without technology. Personalized learning is enabled by smart e-learning systems, which help dynamically track and manage the learning needs of all students, and provide a platform to access myriad engaging learning content, resources, and learning opportunities needed to meet each student's needs everywhere at any time, but which are not all available within the four walls of the traditional classroom. (Wolf, 2010, p. 6)

Our experience implementing the IPL model over the past five years is consistent with Wolf's description. We have found that technology typically plays the following roles in personalized learning:

- Providing immediate, specific, objective feedback on learning that can also serve as a dialogue trail about learning efforts and activities.
- Sustaining motivation by providing choices of relevant content, customized learning pathways, and varying levels of difficulty.
- Capturing real-time data that support analysis and tracking of student learning. For many activities, technology can

be used to record and share results immediately, helping teachers to analyze areas of struggle and intervene quickly before confusion and misconceptions set in.

- Supporting student reflection on learning strategies, challenges, ideas, and experiences and facilitating the sharing of reflections with others.
- Seeking out, identifying, and contributing additional learning content and tools to support individual and group learning. When students bring additional information and their own discoveries to bear on their learning, their sense of commitment to and ownership of the learning grows.
- Tracking progress on learning goals, action plans, student achievement, and assessments. Technology can place these activities in the hands of learners as well as educators and parents, thus supporting shared responsibility and ongoing student-teacher collaboration.
- Providing multiple means for learners to acquire, express, and engage with information and participate in a variety of assessment activities, leveraging principles such as Universal Design for Learning (Hall, Meyer, & Rose, 2012).
- Supporting skills practice and knowledge acquisition. Well-constructed applications can support learners to engage in independent practice with real-time feedback and track progress related to consistency and automaticity.
- Communicating and collaborating with others. Technology can facilitate ongoing dialogue, questioning, information sharing, and problem solving among learners or with adults without necessitating face-to-face contact.
- Introducing and supporting learning challenges and simulations. Students can be given the freedom and flexibility to engage in a variety of interesting activities that also generate a wide range of learning outcomes.
- Exploring and learning from perspectives beyond geographic boundaries. No longer must learners depend solely

on textbooks, field trips, or the knowledge of educators to explore and understand other perspectives. Technology allows them to see the marvels of the world, speak in real time with experts from around the corner or around the globe, and explore history from the perspective of others who have vastly different views and experiences.

• Supporting embedded assessments in the form of simulations, virtual worlds, augmented realities, and game-based performances. Technology can support assessment activities that range far beyond traditional paper-and-pencil tests. Well-constructed assessments can help learners to build clarity and coherence regarding what they are learning, thus adding value beyond simply measuring progress.

ACTIVITY

The Readiness for Change Rubric

Time: 30 minutes

Type: Reflective

Who: Administrative team

Difficulty: 2 out of 5

This gets you: A sense of how ready your school is to start designing for and implementing personalized learning. Don't worry if you find that most of your responses fall in the "not in place" category. The key is to understand where you and your school are now and where you may need to start.

Keep in mind: Just because you're ready as a leader to implement personalized learning doesn't mean that your staff is ready. Be honest as you complete this rubric. You may find that you need to spend additional time on prerequisite activities before embarking on implementation. Every school's journey is different. The key is just to get started.

Rating system values:

1 – Not in place

2 – In process

3 – Substantially in place

4 – In place (implemented)

5 – Ready for adjustment or refinement

We have developed a clear and compelling picture of the need for educational change.	1	2	3	4	5
We have made a commitment to organizational change.	1	2	3	4	5
We have carefully and thoroughly examined the assumptions underlying the current system of educating learners and identified those that need to be altered or abandoned.	1	2	3	4	5
We have identified potential action steps in response to the needs and pressures for change.	1	2	3	4	5
We have developed new assumptions regarding how the system works or can work.	1	2	3	4	5
We have communicated the needs, pressures, and options for change throughout the school.	1	2	3	4	5
We are dedicated to nonlinear, fundamental change—not incremental change.	1	2	3	4	5
We have developed new ideas and approaches related to instructional practices and student learning.	1	2	3	4	5

We have shared information about shifting the system toward personalized learning with key staff.	1	2	3	4	5
School leaders understand personalized learning and can clearly articulate why it's being implemented.	1	2	3	4	5
The principal understands personalized learning and can clearly articulate why it's being implemented.	1	2	3	4	5
Educators understand personalized learning and can clearly articulate why it's being implemented.	1	2	3	4	5

If you indicated mostly 3s and above, your school is ready to start implementing the personalized learning model. If your school is not ready, in addition to reading on, be sure to

- Clarify your mission and vision statements to support personalized learning.
- Investigate examples of and explore research on personalized learning.
- Facilitate overview sessions to communicate the need for change (and the direction that the change will take) to staff. Explain that school is about meeting the needs of students, not adults, and that you will all be undertaking this journey together—with room for trying new things and the understanding that not everything will immediately work out.

Create a chart with three columns labeled "Action Step," "Timeline," and "Evidence of Progress" and fill it out with the steps you intend to take to get your school ready for personalized learning.

Reflection Questions

1. How would you compare the learning ecosystem at your school with the descriptions in the vignette at the beginning of the Introduction? What seemed familiar and what didn't?
2. Why is it important for any definition of personalized learning to address the role of learners?
3. What features of personalized learning do you find most compelling? Which ones might already be present in your school?
4. What role does technology play in the learning experiences at your school? To what extent does it contribute directly to improvements in learning?
5. How might technology contribute to learning growth and quality of work in a personalized learning environment?

Actions You Can Take

1. Share the vignette at the start of the Introduction with a group of staff members and discuss the differences and similarities to your school. What benefits do the learning ecosystems described in the vignette offer? How do educator and learner roles and behaviors in the schools observed differ from those in traditional classrooms? How might shifting toward these types of roles and behaviors affect student learning?
2. Ask several colleagues and staff members how they would define personalized learning and listen carefully to what you hear. How do their definitions compare to the one on page 6? How easily can you identify any key differences? Use this information to clarify your thinking about personalized learning and begin discussions about how learning and teaching might change in your school.

3. Take an inventory of the ways in which technology supports learning in your school. To what extent does it replace or reposition traditional pen-and-paper practices? What examples can you identify of technology being used to show learners content and present experiences that were unreachable before? Are learners using technology to acquire knowledge and skills beyond what they're taught by their teachers? Where can you identify opportunities to better leverage technology in pursuit of improved student learning?

4. Develop your own position about the relationship between technology and learning, perhaps committing it to writing. Should you decide to walk the path of redesigning the learning environment in your school, your ability to clearly and consistently articulate the relationship between personalized learning and technology will be crucial to success.

5. Before going any further, take some time to reflect on your commitment to lead. Deciding to redesign the learning environment in your school to focus on learners and learning will require energy, stamina, focus, creativity, flexibility, and learning of you and your organization. You may be standing at a crossroads in your career and journey as a leader. The choice you make likely will have implications far beyond what you can imagine today. You do not have to decide now, but keep this dilemma in mind as you read further. Continue to ask yourself what is right for you and for the learners and educators whose futures depend on your choice.

1

Assumptions, Logic, and Levers: Changing Practices

As we continued to push new models, it was clear that everybody had an assumption about school: teachers, parents, principals, and students. These assumptions were so powerful that any changes were always met with a need for assurance that things would be "better." This was the very moment that became the tipping point. I asked just one question: "Can you tell me about a time where you were part of an effective learning experience?" First of all, everyone had a story, but even more importantly, everybody could articulate a powerful personalized learning experience.

—Ryan Krohn, assistant superintendent for
curriculum and instruction/education accountability,
School District of Waukesha, Wisconsin

It's funny how change can sneak up on you in unexpected ways. Our partnership with the Institute for Personalized Learning opened a door that allowed us to dream big—to rethink education as we had experienced it up to this point. We could overhaul our teaching strategies and the environment in which we support students. We were able to take the ceiling off of our teaching and reach our students in ways we never had before.

With administrative support to try new things, we have been able to take risks with our instruction and with our students. We are now free to "fail forward." The power has now shifted from us being the sole deliverers of instruction, to our students giving voice to what that instruction will look like. They are now copilots in our learning journey. The results have been more than we could have expected: Our students are engaged, we are engaged, and the things that our students know and do truly show that they are on the road to being strong 21st century learners.

Now that year 2 of our personalized learning journey is coming to a close, we cannot imagine teaching any other way. We are invigorated. We are passionate. We are continually looking for ways to improve—not for us, but for the greater good of our students.

—Kate Sommerville & Angela Patterson, 5th grade teachers, Swanson Elementary School, Elmbrook School District, Wisconsin

● ● ●

Three hundred years ago, if you were ill and visited a physician, you might have expected to have your blood drawn, but not to be tested—to actually treat your illness. Today we know that bloodletting probably contributed to the deaths of many patients and made many others more susceptible to illness and disease.

Although we might look back now and scoff, bloodletting was based on commonly held assumptions about the best ways to treat illnesses and was considered among the best medical practices of its day. In fact, much research was conducted to determine the conditions under which it should be applied and what other medical procedures might complement it.

Interestingly, there were physicians and researchers even then who questioned the efficacy of bloodletting. Still, the practice continued because it was generally assumed to be the right thing to do. It was only when the medical community discovered the true causes of illnesses and began to apply more effective procedures that bloodletting fell into broad disfavor. It was never entirely abandoned, however: the practice is actually still being used today to treat certain blood-related ailments. The difference is that assumptions underlying its use are now much more sound, making it a very specifically targeted procedure (Greenstone, 2010).

So, what does bloodletting have to do with our practices in education today? It is disheartening to think of the number of school practices that are still supported, reinforced, and even expanded despite having consistently failed a large portion of learners. In many instances, these practices may have been suited to the context and purposes of education when they were first employed over a century ago. But today, when virtually all learners are expected to achieve at high levels, they are inadequate. Like bloodletting, some traditional practices may be effective under specific, limited conditions—and that's all.

The Power of Assumptions

Assumptions, of course, are what we believe to be true. Whether we're conscious of them or not, the assumptions we hold can play a crucial role in how we form our perceptions and develop our beliefs. When our assumptions are correct, they help us to focus on actionable options rather than become distracted by impractical and unworkable solutions. When they are not correct, they confine us to a narrow set of possibilities and prevent us from charting new courses, practicing new behaviors, or setting new goals.

The world has changed enormously since certain existing assumptions about education first took root. For example, there was a time when we could afford to educate only a select few learners at high levels and allow the rest to leave school with relatively low skills, knowing that the lower-skilled workers could still secure jobs that ensured a middle-class lifestyle. Today, most of those jobs are either automated or outsourced abroad. Our current economy requires an ever-growing portion of each graduating class to fill increasingly skilled and complex work roles, yet our schools operate in ways designed to serve an economy that existed 50 or even 100 years ago. Today we know much more about brain development and how people learn, yet we continue to manage schools as though more effort and accountability alone will somehow bridge performance gaps.

When redesigning a school system, we must first examine the assumptions upon which the current system rests and abandon those that are misguided. For example, consider the following assumptions about common school practices:

- **Practice:** Grouping learners by age and moving them through the system in batches.

  Assumption: Students learn at the same rate and are ready for new learning at the same time as others born in the same year.

  Fact: Each student learns at his or her own pace based on level of interest, learning history, maturity, and background knowledge.

  What if . . . we gave students the support they needed to learn at a pace dictated by their individual readiness rather than by their ages?

- **Practice:** Using the same instructional approaches for entire groups of learners.

  Assumption: Ability to keep pace with the class and learn from a set of standard instructional strategies is a good measure of learning aptitude.

  Fact: Not all students learn in the same ways, and teaching them as though they did makes it inevitable that some will be held back when they're ready to move forward while others will struggle to keep up.

What if . . . we gave students the time they needed to learn and the support necessary to learn in the ways that best fit them?

• **Practice:** Waiting for learners to fail repeatedly before providing "remediation."

   Assumption: Failure is inevitable for some, and learners who fail need to be "fixed."

   Fact: We don't have to wait for students to fail repeatedly before adjusting instruction to their learning needs, and "fixing" should begin with the instructional strategies.

   What if . . . students were able to learn the way they learn best from the beginning and could receive the support they need in real time, as they're struggling?

• **Practice:** Attempting to capture learning performance and progress through credits and letter grades.

   Assumption: It isn't necessary to be specific when reporting what students have learned; a general indication of what the educator judges as unsatisfactory, satisfactory, or exemplary is enough.

   Fact: Credits and grades tell us little about the nature and level of current student learning. At best, credits are general indicators of progress, and grades are too often contaminated by factors unrelated to learning.

   What if . . . learners had access to immediate feedback and were able to track their progress against standards in detail and in real time, all of the time?

• **Practice:** Using a system of rewards and sanctions to control student behavior.

   Assumption: Students will not choose to learn without either the promise of rewards or the threat of sanctions.

   Fact: Students show us constantly that they will choose to learn what they see as relevant, purposeful, interesting, and challenging. We only need to watch learners who appear bored and disconnected at school engage in social media, video games, and extracurricular activities to see that they can be motivated to commit deeply. Further, when we send learners the message that we don't believe they will choose to learn without external motivators in place, we communicate that the learning isn't worthwhile on its own.

What if . . . the incentives and supports we offered to students were designed to develop self-regulatory skills and an internally driven commitment to learn?

- **Practice:** Administering standardized tests and assessments that focus almost exclusively on content knowledge.

  Assumption: Knowing names, dates, places, sequences, and formulas is enough.

  Fact: It isn't enough to define learning as simply memorization and recall of information. Technology has made memorization less necessary than it used to be, and much of what we might ask learners to memorize today may no longer be relevant or even accurate in the future. Further, when we allocate significant portions of learning time to low-level activities such as memorization and recall, we waste time that students could dedicate to building skills and learning capacity. These are competencies that will serve learners well in situations where problems are not neatly defined and challenges demand deeper understanding and creative, flexible approaches.

  What if . . . learning and teaching were focused on building the learning skills and capacity necessary to thrive in a rapidly changing future, with specific content serving to provide context for learning application?

The Logic of Personalized Learning

We know that learning begins with attention. Unless we are able to find relevance and draw connections, we are bound to let opportunities for learning pass us by. Sinatra (2000) describes the learning process as autonomous, active, and self-constructed. Every day, we encounter innumerable stimuli that have the potential to result in learning. Because it is impossible to take in everything, we learn to pay attention to the stimuli that seem to hold meaning or relevance for us. This dynamic has important implications for the work of stimulating and nurturing learning in schools.

The traditional, "industrial" model of learning was designed to provide substantially the same learning stimuli to everyone in the class at the same time. Some learners would find a reason to pay attention—due to personal interest, perhaps, or because they wanted to please the teacher, or maybe because they knew they needed to do well to be allowed on the football team—and others wouldn't. Such an outcome may have been acceptable in an era when most students were destined for traditional factory jobs, but today we need an educational system capable of supplying *all* students with a strong academic foundation. Our society requires citizens who can adapt to rapidly changing environments, think creatively, and critically analyze problems. Rather than a one-size-fits-all approach, we need an educational system built on the understanding that *all learning is personal* and with the flexibility to engage learners where they *are* rather than where the lesson, curriculum, or pacing chart assumes they *should be*.

Unless students are open and ready to learn, they aren't likely to do it. The school leader's challenge is to support educators as they create the conditions for *individual* learners to notice, engage with, and learn new content and skills. We can no longer be satisfied simply with sowing information like a farmer and hoping that the seeds of knowledge will take hold. We must actively ensure that students make frequent connections when learning and engage deeply as they learn. Unless we understand and accept the logic of this premise, there is no compelling reason to personalize the learning experience (see Figure 1.1).

Figure 1.1
Personalized Learning Logic Model

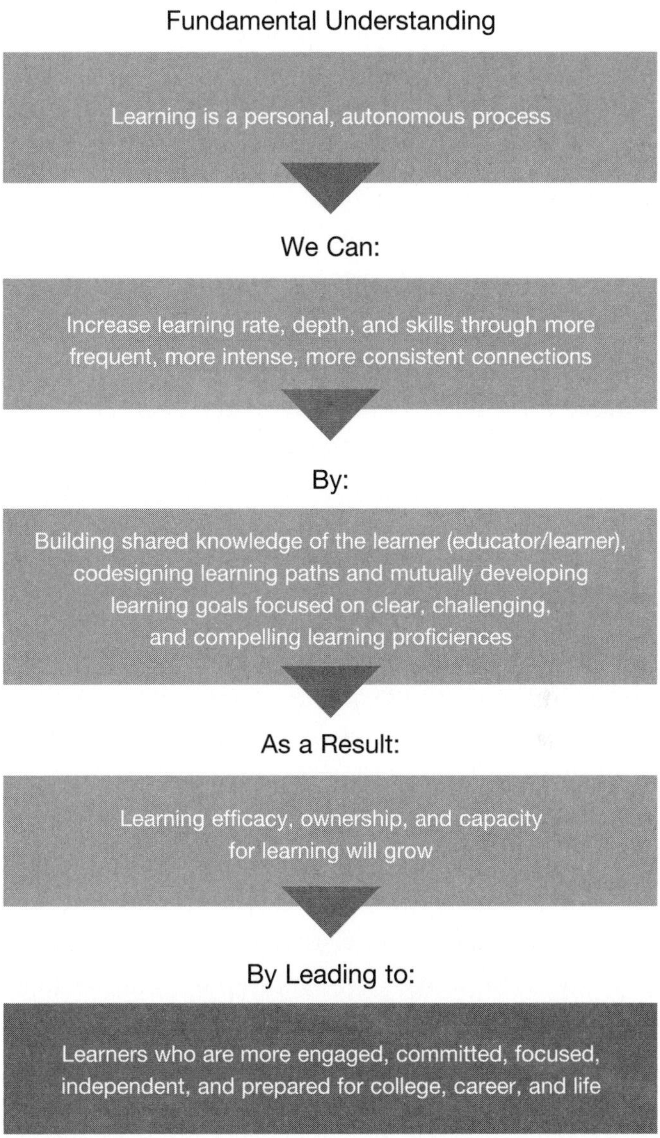

Fundamental Understanding

Learning is a personal, autonomous process

We Can:

Increase learning rate, depth, and skills through more
frequent, more intense, more consistent connections

By:

Building shared knowledge of the learner (educator/learner),
codesigning learning paths and mutually developing
learning goals focused on clear, challenging,
and compelling learning proficiences

As a Result:

Learning efficacy, ownership, and capacity
for learning will grow

By Leading to:

Learners who are more engaged, committed, focused,
independent, and prepared for college, career, and life

By increasing the frequency, intensity, and consistency of the connections students form with content, knowledge, and skills while also minimizing irrelevant stimuli, educators can have a dramatic effect on student learning. The intensity of the learning experience will be determined by students' levels of psychological readiness and emotional states, just as consistency in making connections will be determined by their levels of readiness, pace, and existing skills. When measuring student progress, we must do so against clear, compelling, and worthy proficiencies. Students will have little reason to commit unless the learning is challenging, purposeful, and ultimately useful. Given that *learning starts with the learner,* any connections that students make will be based on their experiences, interests, goals, and needs. The first thing we as educators must do to nurture these personalized connections is to really know our learners. Only then are we in a position to share knowledge and understanding with them.

Employing the Right Levers

Though there have been myriad changes to our education system over the years—increased accountability, calendar and schedule changes, school choice, merit pay, ability grouping, smaller schools, increased testing, higher standards—few have resulted in improved outcomes for all learners (Payne, 2008). Decades of efforts have failed to meet the needs of our society. We deserve a system with the capacity to address current and emerging aspects of learning such as flexible thinking, systems awareness, and effective problem framing that are increasingly necessary for success in the world at large.

The good news is that we are beginning to understand just why previous approaches haven't worked and what we might do to change the situation. Recently, my colleague Tony Frontier and I completed a review of over 40 years of research on school improvement initiatives and created a simple framework to determine the potential efficacy of efforts to improve learning (Frontier & Rickabaugh, 2014). Our framework identifies the following five levers for change to which policymakers and educational leaders typically have access when trying to make system improvements:

1. **Structures:** Organizational options, tools, and logistics
2. **Samples:** Student grouping options
3. **Standards:** Expectations and progress benchmarks
4. **Strategies:** Interactions that produce learning
5. **Self:** Student and teacher beliefs about learning and their roles in learning

Each of these five *S*s holds varying levels of promise for supporting significant and sustainable improvements in learning. Interestingly, the levers most often employed by legislators, policymakers, and even some educational leaders are those with the least potential to affect student learning.

Lever 1: Structures. This lever refers to the manipulation of structural elements such as calendars, schedules, class sizes, grade configurations, improved facilities and equipment, and even technology to improve performance. Simply changing the structure of the educational system can help to support more powerful change levers, but is on its own a largely ineffective way to improve learning. Adjusting schedules to ensure adequate time for learning may be well and good, but unless learners are engaged in highly effective instructional activities, it won't improve learning outcomes (Zepeda & Mayers, 2006). Similarly, research shows that technology offers little benefits over traditional instructional activities unless it is strategically employed in the service of rich, effective learning (Tamim et al., 2011).

Lever 2: Samples. Many change initiatives have also relied on this lever, which posits that learning will increase if we group students strategically for instruction, whether by ability, age, interest, gender, or current performance. However, there is little evidence that student grouping by itself leads to significant and sustained improvement in learning performance (Pahlke, Hyde, & Allison, 2014; Worthy, 2010). It is true that certain groupings can enhance or impede the effects of instructional strategies, but grouping strategies are not themselves drivers of improved student learning.

Level 3: Standards. Many educators and policymakers assume that simply raising or establishing new standards will result in improved learning, but a review of the research shows this is not true (Loveless, 2012). Standards can play a role by making it clear what students are expected to know and be able to do, but to make a significant difference in learning outcomes, we must align intended learning outcomes, instructional strategies, and teacher and student roles in the learning process.

Lever 4: Strategies. This lever is more powerful and dependable than the previous three. Well-chosen instructional strategies can help teachers to engage students, nurture their learning, and improve their performance. Examples of powerful, research-based strategies include those offered by Marzano (2007), Hattie (2009), and Hall and colleagues (2012).

Lever 5: Self. This is potentially the single most powerful lever for improving learning outcomes. It involves changing students' and teachers' existing beliefs about learning and their roles in the learning process. If educators see teaching as simply the transference of knowledge, then student learning will be confined to the educators' expertise rather than encompassing a wide range of resources that might be most impactful for learners. Similarly, if students confine their role in learning to following adult directions and learning to gain the approval of others, they have little incentive to become skilled, independent learners.

All five of the above levers play unique roles in driving and supporting significant change in our education system. The key to deploying them successfully is to tap the power that each can bring to improvement efforts.

What We Have Known for a Long Time About Personalized Learning

Many assume that personalized learning is a new, untested approach. In fact, it is among the oldest methods of learning—Socrates employed it centuries ago. More recently, Benjamin Bloom proved many of the benefits and opportunities embedded in personalized learning (Bloom, 1984). Bloom and his graduate students at the University of Chicago conducted a series of studies in small groups and occasionally one-to-one, using mastery learning strategies and other techniques similar to those employed in personalized learning, to see if they could lift the learning of *all* students significantly beyond the level typically experienced in traditional classrooms.

The research uncovered some amazing results. Learners in the studies who received initial instruction in small groups using learner-focused strategies at a pace calibrated to match their readiness and who were offered feedback and support when necessary improved their average performance by two standard deviations—a 98 percent improvement. This level of performance was comparable to the top 20 percent of learners in traditional classrooms. The research also found that student engagement with learning ranged consistently between 85 and 95 percent across all ages of learners—an amazingly high level given that the average for U.S. students is in the 80 percent range for elementary school, 60 percent for middle school, and 40 percent for high school (Gallup, 2013).

You may be wondering why, if these results are so strong, we haven't been using Bloom's strategies for the past three decades. The answer is that Bloom couldn't find a way to scale the approach to reach all learners, and his instructional approach was too resource-intensive to fall solely on educators. But he showed that personalized learning *works*—that it's not a matter of *if,* but of *how.* Thirty years ago, Bloom didn't have access to the technology available today. Learners no longer must depend on educators to introduce them to all new content or support all learning activities, nor must they rely solely on teacher-generated resources and assessments. Today we have a wide array of potential tools, supports, resources, and strategies to support learners on a personal learning path.

We also know more about how students learn than we did 30 years ago. We have more strategies for engaging and supporting them and we are learning more every day. We no longer need to ask, "Can personalized learning work?" Rather, we need to ask how we will make it work at scale.

ACTIVITY

Most Powerful Learning Experience

Time: 10+ minutes

Type: Reflective

Who: Implementation team

Difficulty: 2 out of 5

This gets you: Thinking about what's important to you and your staff as learners and what the implications are for selecting common themes when designing new experiences for younger learners.

Keep in mind: This is a great activity to start a team meeting!

Ask participants to reflect on their most powerful K–12 learning experiences and answer the following questions:

- What was notable about the teacher?
- What was notable about the work?
- What was notable about the learning?
- How were you different in that situation compared to most days?

Allow the group time to reflect and discuss in pairs. Invite individual participants to share. Listen for elements such as clarity of recall, the effect of the experience on participants' lives, the emotional content of their recollection, and the power of the connection that participants made with both the learning and teachers involved. Facilitate a conversation around these elements and discuss how the experiences we offer students every day can have a lifelong effect, regardless of whether we know it or not. How can we create the conditions for such learning experiences?

Reflection Questions

1. How can the assumptions we make prevent us from seeing opportunities that may be in front of us? Which of the assumptions discussed in this chapter have led you to question your thinking and practice?
2. Do you hold certain assumptions about learning that you need to examine and perhaps change to allow you and your school to improve?
3. How do you coach your staff to help learners make connections and see their learning as meaningful, purposeful, and useful?

4. To what extent and where are learner-based goal setting, action planning, progress monitoring, and demonstrations of achievement present in your school? How visible are these processes to learners?

Actions You Can Take

1. Use the five-lever framework to analyze an initiative or reform attempt you tried recently. What levers were involved and what potential did they hold to deliver the outcome you intended? Now think about redesigning the learning ecosystem of your school. Which levers will you engage first, and which ones can be left for deployment later in the process?

2. Review the assumptions discussed in this chapter and note those that are driving educational practices in your school. Share the list with colleagues who you think might be willing to consider a new approach to learning and teaching and discuss with them how current assumptions and associated practices might be serving learners poorly.

3. At the next staff meeting, ask educators to raise their hands if they have students in their classes who are capable of learning at a faster pace than they currently are. Then ask if they have learners who would benefit from learning at a slower pace. Ask teachers what they're doing to meet the needs of these learners. Conclude by asking if anyone would be interested in exploring ways to redesign the learning environment to allow more flexibility for learners without increasing the workload of educators.

4. Conduct an informal survey of students at your school about their experiences. Sample questions might include: How often do you find that the pace of learning is too fast or too slow in your classes? What do you think the school values most—good grades or good learning? How easily

and quickly can you get the support you need when you struggle to learn something? How often are you invited, encouraged, and supported to think and act for yourself rather than wait to be told what to do?

5. As you visit classes and listen in on lessons, ask yourself whether the purpose of learning is clear and compelling and what could be done to make it more so. Does the learning seem to have lasting value? Will it serve learners well 20 or more years from now? As you debrief lessons with staff, explore these questions and discuss how they might make a more compelling case for students to invest their attention and energy in learning.

6. If there are staff members in your school who already set personal learning goals with students, schedule time to visit with them. Probe what prompted them to take this approach, what benefits they've seen, and how they would improve their current practice if given the opportunity and adequate support. What aspects of their current practice will you want to reinforce and how might you coach them to improve? Consider how these practices might be expanded to benefit more learners in your school.

2

The Honeycomb Model

As an organization, we used the honeycomb model to help establish our understanding of the components of personalized learning. This understanding has evolved over time, as has the diagram, which has also provided our organization with benchmark criteria to gauge our growth toward a more personalized learning system.

—Randy Daul, principal, Asa Clark Middle School

Mr. Thompson, the principal at Silver Valley Middle School, and his staff had for several months been discussing potential new ways to engage students—not only to increase test scores but to revitalize the process for learning and teaching to be more collaborative and personalized. They had heard of other schools that had redesigned their learning ecosystems by shifting the roles of learners and educators and were excited to try a similar approach. Despite their enthusiasm, the prospect was a little scary: shifting roles meant disrupting traditions, expectations, routines, and assumptions about what it means to be a learner or educator. Still, the Silver Valley staff saw the promise of an environment where learners were more engaged and committed to their learning and where teachers could spend more time coaching and nurturing learning rather than managing off-task and disruptive behavior. The new approach seemed worth a try, but where should they start? What changes would come first? Were some starting places better than others?

The staff decided to begin making changes at the intersection of learning and instruction and build out from there. As they proceeded, they found ways to align instructional practices, transform the relationships between students and teachers, secure new technology, rework their grading system, and reallocate space and staffing across the school. Looking back two years later, Mr. Thompson observed that it was the decision to start at the center and build out that had the greatest effect on Silver Valley's success. Since staff began implementing the changes, students had become much more engaged and enthusiastic, misbehavior and discipline incidents had decreased dramatically, test scores had risen, and everyone's expectations for themselves and each other had grown considerably.

Starting at the Center

We know that learning starts where learners are—not where the pacing guide says they should be, where the lesson we want to teach is, where we are, or where we would like the learners to be. This observation may seem obvious, yet on most days in most schools we prepare lessons based on factors other than what each learner needs and is ready to learn. If we hope to help *all* learners find success, we need a new approach—one that taps the potential of the most underutilized resource in most traditional classrooms: *the students themselves*. Amazingly, this approach adds almost nothing to the cost of instruction. However, it does require us to think differently by enjoining us to start at the center—the intersection of learning and teaching—rather than the outer edges.

The power of our model of personalized learning grows out of three interdependent components:

- A detailed understanding or profile of each learner,
- A set of clear and compelling proficiencies toward which each learner is progressing, and
- Collaboration with each learner to construct a customized learning path.

Our model of personalized learning is graphically represented as a modular structure that resembles a honeycomb (see Figure 2.1). The approach employs the *Self, Strategies,* and *Standards* levers discussed in Chapter 1, as these levers when employed together have the greatest potential to significantly improve learning outcomes for all learners. The model taps what we know about learning as an autonomous process: it starts with the learner and clarifies purpose, offers autonomy, and builds a path to mastery.

Getting Started

At the beginning of the journey toward personalized learning, leaders will want to know how much time it will take to implement the model. Not surprisingly, the answer varies depending on numerous factors, including the readiness of educators involved, the current state of learning and teaching practice in a school, the amount of openness to and support for new approaches, and the level of staff comfort with the change process. The good news is that within a matter of weeks, early results typically are visible in the form of increased engagement and ownership of learning among learners, enthusiasm among educators about the shifts in relationships with students, and new, more effective processes in place to support learning. In a matter of months, we typically see these processes stabilize enough to allow for

Figure 2.1
The Honeycomb

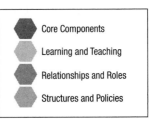

Core Components

Learning and Teaching

Relationships and Roles

Structures and Policies

adjustments and improvements based on early experience and the ideas of teachers and students.

It can take more time and support for learners who have been in the traditional system for a number of years to embrace the experience of learning that is personalized than for those who have less experience with traditional schooling, but the difference can be measured in months rather than years. Educators typically find that implementing the model reminds them of their early years of teaching, when they were first learning their craft and finding a rhythm to their work. Their level of comfort and confidence with new practices typically grows quickly, often in a matter of months.

Scaling beyond the initial group of educators who are leading the way can begin after as little as a semester and usually within a year. Consequently, leaders need to consider early on how to build on the experience and expertise of the initial group, identifying second, third, and subsequent iterations of the implementation process. The time necessary to fully scale the model will vary. Some schools have been able to move from implementation in a few classrooms to the whole school in as few as two or three years, while others have moved more slowly, allowing demand for the new approach to drive expansion. Still other schools have chosen to retain their original approach as an option for those who prefer more structured, adult-driven instruction. Leaders need to think long-term about where implementation will lead from the beginning, lest they build unnecessary barriers to future scaling as demand grows. (See Appendix A for a more detailed description of activities that principals can use to energize and position their schools for personalized learning.)

The Three Core Components of the Model

As Figure 2.2 shows, there are three core components at the center of the honeycomb: learner profiles, customized learning

Figure 2.2
Core Components

paths, and proficiency-based progress. It is here that redesign of the learning and teaching ecosystem begins; these three core components represent the innovation platform that supports the rest of the model. Other elements within each ring of the honeycomb can be approached in a variety of sequences depending on preference and readiness. Though it can be tempting to jump to the familiar practices of the outer ring, we have consistently found that starting at the core and building out is crucial for developing the capacity of learners and educators and changing the way they relate to and engage in their learning.

Learner Profiles

Learner profiles (see Figure 2.3) are cocreated by educators and learners and composed of rich, current information regarding each student. They typically include at least four dimensions:

Figure 2.3
Learner Profile

FRAME 1	FRAME 2
Demographic Data	Academic Status
• General identification • Family/living arrangements • Family history of formal learning • Other information	• Test scores • Progress data • Formative/Interim assessments • Current academic goal(s)

FRAME 3	FRAME 4
Learning-Related Skill Set	Potential Learning Drivers
• Skills • Habits • Dispositions • Current nonacademic goal(s)	• Current preoccupations • Hopes for the future • Factors that propel learning • Other goals

- **Demographic data.** These include current living circumstances and related information, learning history, and potential barriers and existing supports for learning (e.g., IEPs, 504 plans). This information represents the context for the learning to come. By knowing the learner as a person and understanding the supports and challenges present in his or her life, we are better able to help him or her make connections and see the utility of learning.

- **Academic status.** This dimension provides an active picture of the learner using a variety of data points, including formative and summative assessments, artifacts of learning,

learning goals, and reflections, helping learners and educators to know what learners may be ready to learn next.

- **Learning-related skill set.** This dimension contains information related to the learner's current capacity to learn: the learning tools, habits, strategies, and skills the learner possesses that support effective and increasingly independent learning.
- **Potential learning drivers.** These are insights regarding the learner's aspirations, potential motivational hooks, current career plans, and other factors that might affect his or her commitment to learning.

Proficiency-Based Progress

Proficiency-based progress and supporting standards represent what learners are asked to learn. Standards provide clear targets for learning and help to drive intermediate learning goals and expected outcomes. This component articulates what students will learn, how deep or broad the learning will be, and what will be measured. Student progress toward the standards is based on growing mastery, not seat time. Importantly, learning progress does not have to follow a single path: where practical, students are given choices regarding the sequence of learning, standards-aligned content and skills to learn, methods and resources to employ, and even how to document and assess learning progress. Regardless of the approach learners take, standards are challenging and compelling, and meeting them will prepare students both for future learning and for later success in their academic, professional, and personal lives.

Customized Learning Paths

Customized learning paths allow learners to codesign their learning with educators rather than simply comply with the directions and expectations of adults. This component is designed to help learners take ownership of their learning, find greater meaning and purpose, and become increasingly independent in their learning skills.

Step 1: Develop personal learning goals. The teacher and student work to develop short-, intermediate-, and long-term personal learning goals. Expected outcomes must be specific and aligned so that the student can see a clear path forward.

Step 2: Select activities and resources to support learning. The teacher and the student suggest activities and resources to use in meeting the student's personal learning goals. The teacher suggests what he or she can offer (e.g., learning activities, useful resources), and the student does likewise (e.g., collaborating with classmates on specific tasks, locating apps to support learning).

Step 3: Identify progress markers. The teacher and student identify markers that show progress toward meeting each learning goal. Progress toward markers typically is measured and noted through the use of formative assessment data and helps learners to focus on learning progress rather than simply what activities and tasks they are working on. Progress markers also allow the teacher and student to determine whether changes in the learning path may be necessary to ensure accomplishment of each goal.

Step 4: Define how the learning will be demonstrated. The final step in constructing customized learning paths is defining how learning will be demonstrated. Early on, students often are inclined to defer completely to educators on assessment matters, but as they commit to and work toward their learning goals, they become better able with educators to identify learning demonstrations and other representations that serve as appropriate and useful assessments.

The process of cocreating learning paths helps students to develop key life skills. The discipline and organization that learners employ in planning their learning will serve them well long after they leave school to pursue lifelong endeavors.

The three foundational elements of the honeycomb model position us to launch and support the design of a very different learning ecosystem than most of us experienced in our formal education. The honeycomb model not only places learners at the center, but encourages them to collaborate on designing, monitoring, supporting, and investing in the learning process alongside educators. The result is a powerful dynamic that invites learners to commit to learning rather than settling for compliance.

Learning and Teaching

The ring of cells surrounding the three core components in the honeycomb model (see Figure 2.4) builds on the core components by adding powerful learning and teaching strategies to help learners accelerate and deepen their learning. These strategies draw on the information in the learner profile, focus on the learning defined by standards and personal learner goals, and help students to make their learning plans real and bring their learning goals within reach. The research-supported practices in this ring of cells are not especially uncommon in traditional approaches to instruction, but here they are applied at the time and in a manner that best serves the personal learning needs of each learner rather than just the class as a whole.

These are the 10 teaching and learning strategies presented in the honeycomb model:

1. **Standards-guided learning.** This strategy reinforces the role of standards in defining the direction and progress of key learning concepts and skills. Standards guide collaboration between students and teachers and become the focus of learning. Students understand the specific standards toward which they are working, use them to guide their learning, and can articulate what meeting the standard will entail. The role of all other strategies in the

Figure 2.4
Learning and Teaching

second ring of the model is to help students meet agreed-upon standards.

2. **Personal learning goals.** The direction established by standards provides a context for each learner to set, plan, and achieve personal learning goals. By establishing and working toward goals that students have had a voice in creating and that are aligned to standards, student achievement increases (Hattie, 2009; Duckworth, Peterson, Matthew, & Kelly, 2007).

3. **Learner voice.** Closely associated with personal learning goals is the role of learner voice. When students have opportunities to share their perspectives, participate in making decisions, set goals, and take ownership of their

progress, their commitment to and confidence in learning grow. Learner voice can play a powerful role in a variety of activities, from setting school rules and constructing learning communities to advocating for resources and learning supports (Mitra, 2008).

4. **Learner choice.** Related to learner voice, this is the practice of providing real, significant, and authentic choices for learners about their learning, the learning environment, and the strategies and approaches that they will use. The truth is that every time a learner has the opportunity to make a choice, he or she creates a unique learning path. Allowing for learner choice not only builds greater commitment to learning among students but also positions them to learn from the outcomes of their choices. As a result, learners become increasingly savvy about the choices they make and aware of the consequences that different choices may present (Stefanou, Perencevich, DiCintio, & Turner, 2004).

5. **Multiple instructional methods and modes.** Obviously, learners vary in their preferences and responsiveness to different methods and modes of instruction. Certainly, direct instruction will be in this mix of options, but the methods and modes might also include digital and virtual learning options, collaboration with peers, and text and video analysis, among many others (Hall et al., 2012).

6. **Cultural responsiveness.** This strategy recognizes that today's learners come from a variety of backgrounds and cultures and that learning and teaching conditions that recognize, accept, and integrate culture as a part of learning lead to better results (Rajagopal, 2011). Culture might be reflected in the content employed to support skill development or incorporated in learner-generated projects and activities that allow students to express themselves through their identities. Further, learners are encouraged to integrate their cultural traditions,

background knowledge, and life experiences to support and generate new learning, and students' cultures are recognized as bringing value to the school and contributing to a sense of connectedness and inclusion.

7. **Rapid-cycle feedback.** A variety of research has reinforced the power of high-quality feedback to support and increase learning. Beyond being descriptive, objective, specific, and connected to learning goals, feedback must also be timely to have the greatest positive impact (Black & Wiliam, 1998; Hattie, 2009; Petty, 2009). This strategy recognizes the importance of providing learners with feedback as promptly as is practical so that they can reflect, learn, and apply it to subsequent learning trials.

8. **Customized responsive instruction.** In contrast to the traditional approach in which the teacher presents a lesson, provides students with opportunities to practice, and then moves on to assess the learning, this strategy asks teachers to first discover what kind of instruction each student needs, taking into account his or her individual readiness, strengths, needs, and interests (Hattie, 2012).

9. **Assessments for/of/as learning.** Assessment activities in the honeycomb model play a variety of roles. Assessments *for* learning—formative assessment—occur, formally and informally, throughout the learning cycle. The results of formative assessments let teachers and learners know what progress has been made, what next steps are appropriate, and whether and when it is time for a summative assessment. Assessments *of* learning—summative assessments—typically occur at the end of the learning cycle. There really should be no doubt as to the outcomes of summative assessments if learners and teachers have used formative assessment data to inform learning focus and choices and make needed course adjustments to achieve mastery. In fact, if performance levels on

summative assessments come as a surprise, the first possibility to consider should be whether the assessment is appropriate and accurately reflects what the learner knows. Assessments *as* learning are those that double as learning experiences and evidence of learning—usually classroom activities of some sort. For example, when students teach peers what they have just learned, they are demonstrating their learning while also increasing their own level of coherence and understanding about it. These types of assessments are often formative but can also be summative (Ontario Ministry of Education, 2010).

10. **Progression toward deeper learning.** Deep learning that students have thoroughly integrated, applied, and used to generate even more learning is of greater value than simple memorization. Learning and teaching activities in the honeycomb model are aimed at developing increasingly sophisticated thinking about and use of concepts, ideas, or skills. The goal is to drive learning to increasingly deep levels and support learners as they investigate, analyze, integrate, and create using that learning. Assessment methods associated with deep learning tend to consist of producing and demonstrating things rather than traditional paper tests (Jensen & Nickelsen, 2008).

To the left and right of the second ring of cells, readers will note that there are six vacant cells. These spaces are meant to recognize that what we know about powerful, personalized learning is still evolving and probably always will. We have continued to revise the honeycomb in response to what we have learned and intend to continue to do so.

Relationships and Roles

As we move farther out from the center of the honeycomb, we come to the ring of cells representing relationships and roles (see Figure 2.5). Interestingly, in the early stages of creating the model, we assumed that the changes necessary to transform the learning and teaching ecosystem would occur largely at the educator level—they would engage learners differently, collaborate more intensely, and generate better results. However, as we watched, listened, and engaged learners in conversation, we discovered that the greatest power of the model lies in repositioning learners in the process. Teachers have to be willing to

Figure 2.5
Relationships and Roles

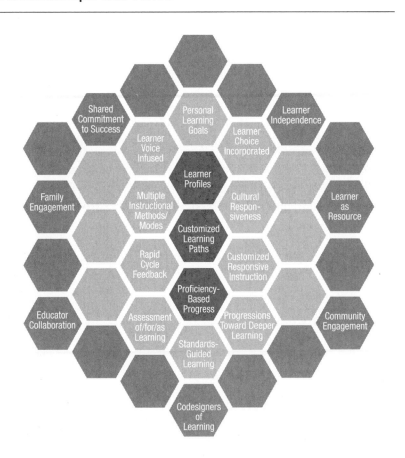

release some measure of control within the learning environment; they must trust learners and position them to play an active and substantive role in mapping, planning, and moving their learning forward.

Magic happens when students realize that they can have a more influential role in their own learning and that they aren't simply vessels to be filled with knowledge possessed by the teacher. They can be codesigners and co-owners of their learning. And when educators realize this as well, they begin to see *learning,* rather than *teaching,* as the key measure of their success. This insight leads educators and students to work together as a team, with educators moving away from roles as dispensers of information and toward roles as mentors, coaches, and supporting resources for learning. This shift is represented in the model by the following cells:

Learner independence. An overarching goal of personalized learning is to develop learners' skills, knowledge, and understanding so that they can succeed in the world long after they've graduated. Consequently, we need to give learners opportunities to make important choices and deal with consequences in ways that build decision-making skills. By encouraging curiosity and a desire to understand, we can prepare learners to stay connected in a world that is rapidly changing. And by giving them opportunities to plan, build, and assess their own learning, we make them less dependent on others and on formal structures to guide their learning. In the end, our job as educators is to reduce learners' dependence on us so that our roles are no longer crucial to their learning success (Mynard & Sorflaten, 2002).

Learner as resource. Traditionally, teachers prepare instruction based on the curriculum and associated units. Unfortunately, this approach is inconsistent with what we now know about learning (Sinatra, 2000). Remember: Learning starts where the learners are, not where we want them to be or where the curriculum imagines them to be. Students begin the process of learning by connecting new knowledge to what they already know, understanding and valuing the purpose of what they are learning, and aspiring to master new knowledge. If we want all learners to be successful, we need to start where they are and position them as their own greatest asset for learning rather than as objects of educators' preset, prescheduled lessons. When we take this approach, we reinforce the importance of learners' roles in their own success, we communicate respect for them as people, and we invite them to invest in themselves rather than simply comply with our wishes and expectations.

Codesigners of learning. When we think of learners as resources for their learning, we do not have to stretch far to see the value of their codesigning learning experiences with educators. After all, they know what interests them, they need to see the purpose of what they are asked to learn, and they often have insights as to how they might approach learning tasks. The learner profile we discussed earlier can play a key role in identifying what students are ready to learn, what approaches have been successful for them in the past, and what skills and strategies they might employ to increase the likelihood of success. When combined with educators' knowledge, skills, and experience, learners' contributions can make a powerful difference in determining what they will commit to learn, how persistent they will be in the face of learning-related struggles, and how much pride and ownership they will experience.

Shared commitment to success. When educators and learners see students as key resources to their own learning and appreciate the interdependence between their roles, they develop a shared commitment to success. When learners see teachers as their best advocates and teachers understand that they will not succeed unless their students do, both parties are more likely to collaborate with one another when problems arise during the learning process.

Educator collaboration. The honeycomb model invites educators to share insights, strategies, problems, and solutions with each other. Collaboration allows educators to learn from each other and share ideas and resources effectively and efficiently. Admittedly, some educators struggle with the skills necessary to successfully collaborate with peers and need opportunities to learn and practice those skills, but the benefits are well worth the effort.

Family engagement. A personalized learning ecosystem opens new opportunities for families to be engaged in their children's learning. Families know a great deal about how their children learn best; they know when their children are struggling and becoming disengaged. The combination of an environment with the learner at the center and the ubiquity of new technology invites family engagement. Certainly, families can play the traditional roles of providing support for learning at home, but they can now also review their children's learning goals and activities, track their progress, and even serve as an audience for student demonstrations and performances.

Community engagement. Like families, communities can find it easier to play a more active and influential role in a personalized learning ecosystem than in the traditional system. For many students, being able to see how their learning applies in the world beyond the classroom can provide them with a sense of purpose, build new energy and interest, and even spark a passion for a career. Communities offer rich opportunities to support learning, and community members should be invited to play active roles in nurturing the learning and development of the next generation of citizens.

Figure 2.6 shows the learner-educator relationship in a traditional ecosystem, where educators are expected to transfer their knowledge to learners as dictated by standards and the curriculum regardless of individual readiness. Under this model, if formative assessments show that students aren't learning what's been taught, teachers must do what they can to reteach aspects

Figure 2.6
Changing Relationships

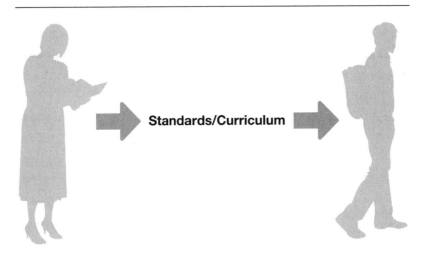

of their lessons while still pushing ahead at a predetermined pace, ultimately administering a summative assessment and assigning grades and moving on whether all learners are ready to or not. Learning often is considered primarily the student's responsibility rather than a direct reflection of the educators' skills, approach, efforts, and partnership with the learner.

Figure 2.7 shows the learner-educator relationship in a personalized learning ecosystem. In this model, educators and learners work together to determine the order, pace, and assessment of learning to meet the dictates of standards and curriculum. Here the assumption is that teachers can only be successful if their students are. Consequently, they are positioned to be strong advocates for student learning rather than serving primarily as planners, presenters, and assessors.

These are some of the shifts educators will encounter as they implement the honeycomb model:

- Planning lessons → designing learning activities
- Providing information → curating learning resources

Figure 2.7
Changing Relationships

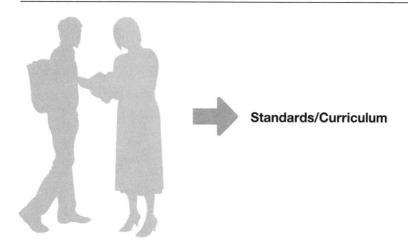

Standards/Curriculum

- Judging performances → advocating, coaching, and working as a partner
- Employing established practices → employing effective learner-focused practices

For learners, shifts include the following:

- Serving as empty receptacles to be filled with the knowledge of others → acting as resources in support of their own learning
- Complying with teacher expectations and directions → codesigning the learning path
- Being skilled at being taught → becoming a skilled learner

As relationships and roles shift, the new learning ecosystem gains the strength and stability necessary to scale beyond isolated pockets of innovation. The emergence of a new vibrant culture makes it safe to take thoughtful risks to increase learning for all learners and provides the support needed to persist when educators struggle, fall back into traditional roles, and become discouraged. Make no mistake: changing practices without changing the culture will make any improvements temporary. As management guru Peter Drucker famously put it, "Culture eats strategy for breakfast."

Structures and Policies

The outer ring of cells in the honeycomb (see Figure 2.8) addresses elements that open avenues to accelerating the change process and are very important to scaling, managing, and sustaining the work. However, these are supporting elements, not driving elements, and should only be addressed and adjusted once the core components, teaching and learning strategies and practices, and roles and relationships of personalized learning have been developed. Unfortunately, in the history of education reform, policymakers and educators have tended to consider elements related to structure, policies, logistics, and resources before considering the elements with the most potential to generate changes in learning. The results have been largely disappointing, not because these elements are irrelevant or cannot contribute to important change, but because they are best able to support and accelerate change once the driving elements are in place. To be clear: structure tends not to be a strong driver of change, but failing to address it at the correct time can slow and even cripple change efforts.

The elements of the structure and policy ring of the honeycomb model are as follows:

Learning-aligned grouping options. Though many educators consider student grouping to be an instructional strategy, grouping alone has not been shown to have a powerful effect on learning (Hattie, 2009; Pahlke et al., 2014). Whether grouping by gender, performance level, or some other criteria, the instructional strategies employed and the role learners and educators

Figure 2.8
Structures and Policies

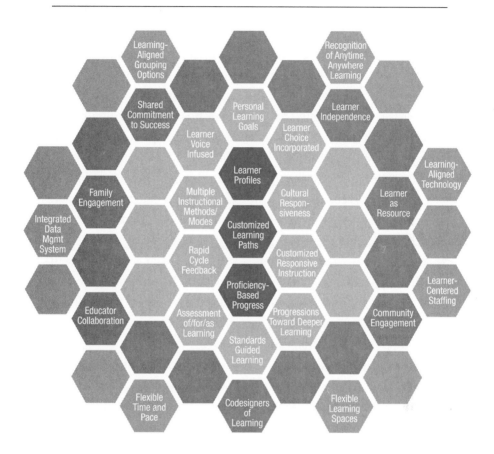

play make the greatest difference, not the makeup of the group. Some grouping strategies can even make learning more difficult, such as the strategy of separating struggling students and thus leaving them without access to models of strong learning among peers. An effective use of this element is to group students according to their readiness. For example, educators might cluster a small group of learners who are ready to address a particular concept and provide them with brief, strategic, and specific instruction. Students who are working on common content or skills might also be clustered together to support each other's learning.

Flexible time and pace. When educators commit to personalizing the learning experience, they also commit to being flexible about the time they allot for learning and allowing students to progress at the pace that best matches their learning needs (Spady & Marshall, 1991). Teachers need to allow students to accelerate or decelerate their pace of learning to ensure that it is rich and deep. Remarkably, when students feel ownership and are given more control over the pace of their learning, we typically see them *accelerate* their learning pace—often dramatically.

Flexible learning spaces. Many education reforms have put this element at their core only to discover that it does little if anything to increase learning (think open classrooms). The key here is that configuration of learning spaces needs to be determined by and aligned to the purpose of instructional practices and needs of the learner.

Recognition of anytime, anywhere learning. In a personalized learning environment with clear, measurable goals, educators support student learning in a variety of places and under a wide range of circumstances. The key, as always, is to focus on the *learning*. The honeycomb model encourages learners to move beyond the classroom to build their skills and expand their knowledge.

Learner-centered staffing. When we place learners at the center of our thinking and practice, we no longer have to restrict ourselves to static teacher-student ratios, and students needn't all be grouped in the same way. In the personalized learning ecosystem, staff assignments can be differentiated according to staff members' particular skills and expertise (and in some cases can be expanded to include noncertified staff).

Learning-aligned technology. Without question, technology has an important role to play in a personalized learning ecosystem. However, as we noted earlier, the presence of technology alone has not been shown to increase learning (Tamim et al., 2011). As with the other elements in this ring of cells, what matters is aligning technology to the needs of learners and the purposes of instruction.

Integrated data management system. A data management system obviously represents an application of technology, and as with the previous element, decisions regarding its use are best made once educators understand the types of data they need to capture and how and by whom they will be used. Regardless, teachers need to be able to collect, analyze, and organize data easily and quickly—and as the personalized learning ecosystem develops, learners increasingly need to understand and use data as well.

The Honeycomb Model in Action

Here is how Jon Tanner, director of technology for the Oregon School District in Wisconsin, described the effects of the honeycomb model:

The honeycomb model has been very useful for us by serving as a conceptual framework to guide the change process. The three core components at the center of the model are the most impactful: teachers can choose to pursue whichever ones best meet their learners' needs—in their own learning environments and without having to coordinate with others.

The model gives teachers concrete strategies that they can implement. The farther from the center of the honeycomb, the more the strategies and tactics depend on external systems, structures, and other people. This means that as the practices are scaled up, they have greater and greater influence. At Oregon we are able to identify which practices teachers or small teams can implement without having to completely change structures or policies. As we expand successful practices, we anticipate that we'll need to integrate changes to elements in the outer ring of the honeycomb model, but only when we've reached the point where the structures or policies begin inhibiting the progress of change.

The honeycomb model has been an excellent nonlinear guide for teachers who are beginning to implement a shift toward personalized learning and offers an effective visual representation of the amount of coordination necessary to pursue certain strategies when scaling from a module to a model and finally to systemic transformation.

As we have shown, the honeycomb model helps teachers chart the learning paths that work best for their students. Once they have addressed the core elements of the model, they can choose to focus on the learning and teaching elements best suited to each student. Relationships and roles will then begin to shift as confidence in new practices grows. As teachers and students become more comfortable in their new roles and begin to understand the implications, the need for structural and policy changes comes increasingly into focus.

ACTIVITY

Personalized Learning Element Matrix

Time: 90 minutes

Type: Reflective

Who: 5 or more staff, administrative team, implementation team

Difficulty: 4 out of 5

This gets you: Thinking strategically about current conditions, resources, and focus at your school and what the best entry points to the honeycomb model may be.

Keep in mind: Don't think you have to tackle the whole honeycomb at once! Start with two or three of the core components and expand from there.

Rating system values:
0 – Nonexistent
1 – Extremely low
2 – Low
3 – Neutral
4 – High
5 – Exceptional

In the following chart, mark the cells in the row for each element according to how well conditions in your environment match the five criteria listed at the top of the chart. When you are finished you will have an initial snapshot of where your organization finds itself relative to the honeycomb model.

	School Plan Alignment	Interest/ Enthusiasm	Access to Expertise	Possibilities for Success	Opportunity for Growth	Total Points
Core Components						
Learner profiles						
Customized learning paths						
Proficiency-based progress						
Learning and Teaching						
Personal learning goals						
Learner voice infused						
Learner choice incorporated						
Multiple instructional methods/modes						
Cultural responsiveness						
Rapid cycle feedback						
Customized responsive instruction						
Assessment of learning						
Assessment for learning						
Assessment as learning						
Progressions toward deeper learning						
Standards-guided learning						

	School Plan Alignment	Interest/ Enthusiasm	Access to Expertise	Possibilities for Success	Opportunity for Growth	Total Points
Relationships and Roles						
Learner independence						
Learner as resource						
Community engagement						
Codesigners of learning						
Educator collaboration						
Family engagement						
Shared commitment to success						
Structures and Policies						
Recognition of anytime, anywhere learning						
Learning-aligned technology						
Learner-centered staffing						
Flexible learning spaces						
Flexible time and pace						
Integrated data management system						
Learning-aligned grouping options						

Reflection Questions

1. What is it about the concept of personalized learning that leads many educators to hesitate before employing it?
2. How do the entry points we choose make a difference to the process of redesigning the learning ecosystem?
3. Consider the most popular prescriptions for reforming our education system. Which of them start by improving the experience of the learner and which start instead by focusing on structures, policies, and logistics?
4. What aspects of the traditional learning environment will you need to abandon to make room for student commitment to and ownership of learning? How difficult will this be?
5. What do you think are the greatest challenges related to scaling personalized learning so that all learners can experience it?

Actions You Can Take

1. At an upcoming staff meeting, ask teachers to identify a student from their classes and write down everything they know about him or her. Then ask them to categorize what they know into four frames: demographic and learning history, current performance, learning skills (study habits, problem solving, collaboration, etc.), and motivators (current interests, achievement orientation, career aspiration, etc.). Discuss the value of this information for reaching students and how we might collect such data on all learners at the school.
2. Convene a group of key staff members to create an inventory of the resources and practices already in place at your school to support construction of the three core components: learner profiles, proficiency-based progress, and

customized learning paths. You are likely to discover that you have more resources than you realize.

3. Depending on the size and configuration of your staff, consider assigning exploration teams to construct prototype models that staff can use to test and gain experience with each of the three core components.

4. Help staff either to select one of the core components to implement or to begin implementing all three.

5. As staff build familiarity and comfort with the core components, work with them to identify personalized learning practices that they might implement beyond the core components. Repeat with each of the successive rings of cells as staff experience and readiness grow.

6. Invite a cross-section of students to join you for a conversation about their learning. Do they see their role as learners as primarily one of complying with teacher direction, or do they feel a personal commitment to their learning? Do they see learning merely as something that is expected of them, or do they see value in it for themselves? Do they see educators as directors and assigners of work or as advocates and guides for learning? Do they see themselves as receptacles to be filled by teacher knowledge or as their own best learning resources? Listen carefully and share what you hear with your staff for further reflection, analysis, and planning.

3

Personalized Learning from the Students' Perspective

You can work with a friend if they have the same goal. That helps because sometimes it's fun to work in a group.

> —Caydence

You get to do things the way you want to, not how your teachers want you to do it.

> —Emily

Personalized learning lets you take risks that you normally wouldn't take. If you get an answer wrong, everyone doesn't have to see that—it's just between you and your teacher.

> —Layla

When you finally complete a goal you get excited.

> —Emily

Oh, we always get excited!

> —Layla

> Students from Amy Pillizzi's class, Kenosha Unified School District, Wisconsin

As simple as it sounds, I want to hear more students talking, show-ing, asking questions to direct their next step. When facilitators (formally known as teachers) talk, you can hear them "ask" rather than "tell." The listen-for is about ownership for the learning.

—Ryan Krohn, assistant superintendent for curriculum and instruction/education accountability, School District of Waukesha, Wisconsin

Ms. Jones and a team of educators from her school have just fin-ished a series of visits to classrooms that are very different from those with which they are familiar. At first they were excited by what they saw: highly engaged students collaborating with classmates, tracking their own progress, and obviously growing in their learning. However, their excitement quickly began to dissipate as they reflected on the dramatic differences in student attitudes and activities occurring in these classrooms compared to their own. They worried about the resistance they would face if they tried creating similar conditions in their schools. Mean-while, they weren't even sure that the model of learning they observed would work with their students. Before long, they had talked themselves out of investing time and energy into trans-forming their existing learning environment.

Ms. Jones and her team fell into the trap of focusing on what they *couldn't* do rather than taking a few steps forward and then building on the progress and experience that they gained. They failed to realize that the classrooms they visited used to look and feel just like theirs—the journey to transform learning starts where we are, not where others find themselves.

The 12 Key Factors of Personalized Learning

It's important to recognize the observable conditions and factors that contribute to an authentic personalized learning environment. Without understanding these key elements, it can be easy to focus too heavily on teacher behaviors or furniture placement rather than on what really matters: the beliefs and behaviors learners bring to and roles they play in their learning. Although not every factor discussed in this chapter will be present in every classroom every minute of the day, the more of them we encounter, the more likely it is that the learning experience of students is truly personalized.

Purposeful Learning

When students understand that their learning serves a valuable purpose, they are more likely to commit to it, persist when it becomes challenging, and retain what they learn (Osberg, 1997; Pink, 2009). Of course, not everything they learn will be immediately applicable to their lives—what matters is that they can see the purpose clearly enough to maintain their commitment and learning momentum. Students who have some say in how and what they learn and perceive that educators have their best interests in mind are generally willing to trust that what they are being asked to learn is worth their effort.

Students in personalized learning ecosystems are more likely than their peers in traditional classrooms to be able to describe exactly what they are learning and how it fits with what they've already learned, addresses key competencies or standards, and serves a greater purpose beyond the classroom. When discussing their work, they are also more likely to point to the processes they are using and the value of their work than to the length, structure, or other compliance-related elements.

The above may sound utopian, but during visits to classrooms that embrace personalized learning, we regularly hear students reference their learning goals, often describing in detail why they selected them, what kind of progress they're making, what activities they're engaging in to support their learning, and how they will demonstrate that they have learned. We frequently watch and listen as students pull up and reference their learner profiles to show us their progress to date.

Learner Efficacy

When students see themselves as capable of overcoming learning challenges, they're more likely to take learning risks and to persist when the work becomes increasingly difficult, drawing lessons and confidence from setbacks rather than immediately abandoning their efforts (Bandura, 1986). Learners with a strong sense of efficacy tend to blame poor strategy or effort rather than lack of ability when they don't succeed (Dweck, 2006). In fact, persistence associated with learner efficacy is an even stronger predictor of life success than intelligence (Duckworth et al., 2007). Educators who want their students to be challenged, to take ownership of their learning, and to become independent learners must nurture a strong sense of self-efficacy (Zimmerman, Bandura, & Martinez-Pons, 1992). In our experience, relative to their peers in more traditional classrooms, students in personalized learning environments are more likely to thoughtfully consider where to allocate their energies for the greatest success and consult with classmates and teachers to overcome challenges—but also are less likely to seek immediate answers, preferring to gain perspective and support for their own efforts.

Observers are often surprised to the point of disbelief when they visit classrooms and see them filled with learners engaged at such a high level. We often hear from visitors, "I have yet to see a single student who is not fully engaged in learning." When we create the conditions to support learners and encourage them to take risks without fear of sanction, they gradually begin to take the work of learning more and more seriously and their confidence grows. We see students in personalized learning ecosystems valuing effective learning strategies over correct answers, effort and focused attention over sporadic and fragmented engagement, helpful tools and resources over answers that don't build understanding. These students are often quick to discuss their struggles and how they overcame them, taking obvious pride in their accomplishments.

Ownership of Learning

When students take ownership of their learning rather than seeing it as something they do primarily to gain adult approval or avoid negative sanctions, it becomes more meaningful to them and they tend to retain it longer (Fletcher, 2008). Students who feel as though they own their learning also tend to take more responsibility for completing tasks and have a higher degree of confidence and pride in their success. They see how learning gives them greater influence over their environment, and they realize it is an asset that cannot be easily stolen, lost, or destroyed.

Students who take ownership of their learning are easy to spot, even in a brief conversation, as they are often eager to share what they have learned, how they have learned it, and how it will help them to find future success. They talk about their learning as an accomplishment rather than a burden. Though they might mention how pleased adults are with their learning, adult approval is not their sole source of pride. These students tend to talk in the first person; we hear them describe what "*I* was able to do," "what *I* now know how to do," and "what *I* plan to do with what I've learned"; they talk about "my" goals and "my" work rather than "the teacher's assignment."

Flexible Pacing

Learning occurs in different ways and at different paces. Remarkably, despite the seemingly obvious implications of this observation, most schools and classes are still organized as though this were not the case: students are grouped in age-based cohorts and marched through lessons, units, and years as though all learning occurred at the same consistent pace. Under these conditions, some students struggle daily to catch up and, too often, will stop trying so that the class can move forward. Others feel bored and disconnected by the slow pace of learning. For most of these learners, being able to learn at a pace matched to their readiness and capacity would translate to increased learning success (Spady & Marshall, 1991).

In a personalized environment, learners are supported as they learn at the pace that works best for them; the measuring stick is *learning* rather than the passage of time. Interestingly, in our experience learners across the performance continuum tend to increase the pace of their learning when given flexibility, at least in part because they feel greater control and find learning challenges realistic and success to be within reach. On the other hand, many students have told us how much they appreciate being allowed to slow down and focus more intently on their work when they need to. Because they no longer feel the need to cover up when they're not able to keep up with the rest of the class, they don't worry as much about how quickly others are progressing.

Learner Voice

All learners have opinions, preferences, and ideas, but their voices have traditionally not played an important role in the classroom—yet when they feel that they are genuinely being listened to, they're more likely to invest in their efforts (Mitra, 2008). Of course, every idea or preference from every student will not always prevail; learners can't always have it their way, and they often aren't aware of the potential implications associated with their perspectives. Although it is important for teachers to listen, take what students have to say seriously, and be responsive, they are ultimately responsible for establishing a balance among the needs and interests of everyone involved.

In a personalized learning environment, students understand that their learning is the most important activity under way. They know that their thoughts and ideas count, even if they cannot always be accepted and carried out. They typically can describe multiple instances in which they have been asked their opinions, been invited to contribute their ideas, and been encouraged to advocate for what is important to them. Inviting and listening to learners' voices supports purposeful learning by nurturing confidence and helping learners to become clearer in their thinking, more articulate in expressing their ideas, and focused on learning that is important and worth pursuing.

Learner Choice

This aspect of a personalized learning environment conveys a sense of respect for what is important to students and supports them as they make responsible decisions. We know that learners are more likely to take responsibility for and commit to choices they personally make than to choices made on their behalf (Kohn, 1993). Of course, learner choice is not unlimited. Choices might be restricted to strategies and approaches that students will use rather than standards and other nonnegotiable aspects of learning. Teachers might offer learners choices from which to pick, invite them to add to an existing list of choices, or ask them to work together to generate a list. Choices have the greatest impact when learners see them as meaningful or authentic. However, not all choices are equal when it comes to learning. Choices that involve, say, classroom procedures might help to build community but will not necessarily improve learning outcomes. By contrast, choices about learning approaches and strategies or even how learners will demonstrate what they have learned have been shown to increase learning (Stefanou et al., 2004).

Learners as Resources

The design of our current education system in many ways is based on the premise that learners are empty vessels to be filled by the knowledge of educators. This perspective assumes that learning is an "outside in" process. Personalized learning relies on an "inside out" approach that positions students to be active agents in the process of constructing learning (Sinatra, 2000). Certainly, students need access to the knowledge of adults, but learning occurs when they can connect that knowledge to what they already know; it is driven as much by student readiness, interest, and motivation as by anything the teacher does. If learners are to serve as resources for their learning, teachers need to help them make connections, find purpose in their learning, and leverage past learning experiences to build new ones. Learners can also be valuable resources to one another's learning, collaborating on learning tasks, sharing what they've learned, and exploring new learning together.

Flexible Learning Spaces

When we think of the physical organization of traditional classrooms, we think of students sitting at desks facing the front of the room. Yet research and experience tell us that not all learning is best nurtured in this arrangement (State of Victoria, 2011). If all students are expected to learn at the same rate and in the same way, rows of desks facing a common direction may make sense, but personalized learning demands greater variety when it comes to learning spaces. Some students may need a quiet space free of distractions in order to concentrate, whereas others may need room to cluster and collaborate on tasks. Still others may need space to stand and move around periodically to think or counter cases of "the wiggles."

Furniture in personalized learning classrooms often includes much more than traditional desks: soft seating, high tables, a central gathering space, and even small cubicles with eye-level separators are all possible options. In all cases, organization of the space must be driven by the needs of learners and of the learning tasks at hand rather than by adult preferences or a simple desire for novelty. Students typically are free to select the spaces that work best for them as long as they don't distract others. Respect for learning, including the learning of classmates, is central to the personalized learning environment. Flexibility in learning spaces also extends to learning that may occur beyond the physical space of the classroom or timeframe of the typical school day: for example, students might be given the option of learning outside the physical classroom or online.

Focus on Commitment

Learning in traditional environments tends to be driven by compliance-based expectations, incentives, and sanctions. Students are told where to be, when to be there, how long they will be there, what they will do, how much they will do, when they must do it, and who will decide whether what they do is satisfactory. Yet we know that rich, meaningful, purpose-driven learning grows out of commitment to learning, not just compliance with adult direction. When students see purpose in their learning, tap areas of interest and passion, have the flexibility to make choices about learning strategies, and can determine their rate of learning, they tend to retain what they've learned longer and to use it much more often (Kohn, 1993; Pink, 2009).

For most students, learning that occurs outside formal settings is more often driven by commitment rather than compliance—and the workplaces for which we are preparing today's students will likely demand levels of commitment far in excess of what they have demanded in the past (Kay & Greenhill, 2012). Teachers are more likely to generate learning when they focus on nurturing and leveraging learner commitment and engaging in as few compliance-driven actions as practical.

When learning is driven by commitment, learners are less likely to ask how many problems they must solve or how long an assignment should be and more likely to focus on understanding and mastery of content and skills. Students across the performance continuum tend to respond with greater enthusiasm and persistence when they engage in work that taps their commitment to learning.

Collaboration

Some might assume that personalized learning requires students to work in isolation from one another, yet the reality is quite different. Although there will always be some learning tasks that are best accomplished alone, collaboration also plays a key role in supporting learning. Quality learning environments include a social dimension (Illeris, 2004), and collaborative learning experiences can strongly enhance the learning process. In a personalized learning ecosystem, students might work alone, in pairs, in small groups, or even as a whole group depending on student preference, the requirements of the task, and the purpose of the learning.

Technology as Learning Support

Many assume that personalized learning and technology-driven learning are the same. The fact is that we can personalize learning without technology—in fact, we have been doing so for centuries. The challenge has been to scale personalized learning environments and make them available to all students. The emergence of rich, flexible technology is bringing what used to seem impossible within reach. Technology now allows students to become more independent, move forward at a pace that matches their readiness, gain immediate feedback, and access a wide variety of resources. The challenge of collecting, organizing, analyzing, and using data to support learning is shrinking. Using technology does not make learning personalized, but technology can make personalization a scalable and sustainable approach.

Growing Learner Independence

Personalized learning environments are organized on the premise that learners should be supported to become their own best teachers. The most important work of educators is to help students develop their skills, knowledge, and learning capacity so that they might succeed without depending excessively on external structures and direction (Mynard & Sorflaten, 2002). In a personalized learning environment, students cocreate their learning paths and take responsibility for their learning; they often talk about their learning goals, the criteria for success, and how they plan to demonstrate what they've learned. For their part, teachers respond strategically to students' questions, being sure to focus on nurturing learning and avoiding undermining learner competence and independence.

Parent and Teacher Reactions

We have heard powerful testimonials from parents and teachers about students' personalized learning experiences. Here just a few examples:

- "Being in a middle school personalized learning program has enabled my daughter to progress in math at her own pace. She has not been bored and has achieved her goals in math much more quickly. She was able to go from a grade-level math student to a double-advanced math student in one school year."

- "This is my daughter's first year in a personalized learning environment. She has progressed so much throughout her first year, and we are very proud of her. She went from a remedial math class to an advanced math class, which makes her dad and me very happy. She not only progressed independently at school, but at home, too. Her teachers are amazing; we couldn't be happier for her. We will recommend the program to anyone who has questions about it. She is going to do a second year, without a doubt!"

- "My daughter Lauren has been in a personalized learning program all year. Because she has struggled in school in the past due to her ADHD, I had initially worried that the program might not provide enough structure for her learning style, but she encouraged her dad and me to find out more about it. After meeting with the teachers and seeing the students in action, I was so impressed by what I saw that we agreed to let Lauren try it. The flexibility of the program has allowed her to work at the pace that's right for her and also motivated her to work harder on presentations and projects. Because she has more freedom to tailor her work to her interests, she is naturally more motivated to work on her school work. I have seen her excited and engaged in her homework more than ever before."

- "Our daughter lives in an age of rapidly evolving social media and technology. We believe that these advances can provide her with new educational resources, new learning opportunities, and new ways to use her knowledge while engaging with the world around her. We've found personalized learning to be the perfect complement to these beliefs. When allowed to independently make choices based on her interests, our daughter was intrinsically motivated to work extra hard. Here's an example: When she was working on a presentation about her youth theater group, she first met with her teacher to determine her educational goals, her approach to the project, and the deadline for completing it. Using her school-issued Chromebook, our daughter used cloud-based presentation software to organize information that she found on the theater group's website as well as from various other online resources. Using her school e-mail address, she contacted a young performer from the group and asked him to join her via Skype during her presentation.

    "Not only did our daughter meet her educational goals with the presentation, but she was able to connect her classroom learning to real-world experience. As technological advances continue to expand our daughter's educational possibilities, the personalized learning program has allowed her to develop qualities such as responsibility and autonomy that will be invaluable to her for the rest of her life."

- "When my students are offered the opportunity of voice and choice within a unit, I notice an immediate change of expression on their faces. You would think I'm hinting that they start smiling and nodding, but that's not it: what I see are 'thinking' faces. I see them wondering, planning, collaborating, decision making—all within seconds of sharing a project idea. Oh, and they smile, too!"

- "My first year working in a math learning center, I had the opportunity to work with a number of our special education students. We wanted an inclusion environment that met all students where they were so we could maximize their learning. One student in particular was a 7th grader at a 4th grade math level and had very negative feelings toward math in general. He had never been successful in math before and felt very strongly that he never would be. Through our conferences, I learned that he had spent the last two years in the regular classroom learning 5th and 6th grade material. He was very unsuccessful because the content he was learning was beyond his current level of understanding. To build his math foundation and his confidence, we started working on the 4th grade content at a pace that was comfortable for him. He was able to increase his math understanding greatly. By the end of his 7th grade year, he was excited to come to math class, wanted to continue working over the summer, and had goals to get to grade level by the end of his 8th grade year. I was just as excited and was very willing to do whatever I could to keep this fire lit. By the end of his 8th grade year, this student was working on pre-algebra content and was able to enter high school in an inclusion setting."

- "By teaching in a personalized learning community, we realize that our shift in teaching has greatly helped our students. We provide students with choice and voice while they work to achieve their personalized academic goals. We have moved education 'beyond the books' by taking necessary steps into 21 century learning via technology. Through professional collaboration and planning, our team focuses on implementing technology in our everyday learning environment. Students are introduced to concepts that are current, relevant, and interesting to each individual learner. These opportunities allow us as teachers to connect with and appreciate our students not only on an academic level, but on a social and emotional level as well. From there, we are able to individualize their academic and social needs, such as cooperation, public speaking, organization, and self-motivation. Learning these skills at an early age helps students to become self-confident, productive, and aware of what it takes to be successful."

ACTIVITY

Look-For Rubric

Time: 15 minutes

Type: Reflective

Who: Comprehensive implementation team

Difficulty: 2 out of 5

This gets you: A quick look at how many conditions are present in classrooms to make the environment truly personalized.

Keep in mind: *This isn't about evaluation!* Just because you don't see evidence of these conditions doesn't mean there is necessarily reason for concern. Not every factor will be present at every moment of the day. Still, the more factors that are in play, the more personalized the learning environment is likely to be.

Rating system values:

1 – Not evident

2 – Partially evident

3 – Evident

Look For	Score
Purposeful learning	
Learner efficacy	
Ownership for learning	
Flexible pace	
Learner voice infused	
Learner choice presented	
Learners serve as resources for learning	
Space for learning flexibility	
Commitment focus	
Collaboration	
Technology supported	
Growing learner independence	

You can also use this tool as you conduct walk-throughs in classrooms, engage teachers in reflection about their practices, and explain to other stakeholders what personalized learning looks like in practice.

Reflection Questions

1. Why have past reform efforts resulted in so little fundamental change in the relationships most learners have with formal learning?
2. How might viewing the learning environment from the perspectives of learners provide us with insights about learning factors other than teacher actions?
3. What practices in your school are preparing learners to be able to learn, unlearn, and relearn as circumstances change and new expectations emerge?
4. Of the 12 look-fors discussed in this chapter, which would a visitor be most likely to see in learning environments in your school? Which do you see having the greatest potential to affect the performance of learners in your school?

Actions You Can Take

1. Share the 12 look-fors discussed in this chapter with some or all members of your staff and discuss which ones are present in your school. What examples exist that could be built upon? Where are there opportunities to learn and add new practices that would place learners closer to the center of learning?
2. The next time you visit a classroom, focus your attention on learners rather than on teacher actions. Is it clear that learners see purpose in the work they are doing? Do they have a sense of ownership of their learning and opportunities for choice? What other elements are present or missing from the learners' perspectives?
3. In follow-up conversations with staff, share the observations and evidence you've collected without judgment or interpretation and then discuss what the information might mean. Consider whether there exist opportunities to

shift focus, redesign activities, and reposition learners to become more committed to their learning.

4. Spend some time with staff members identifying specific aspects or elements on which you want to focus and improve practice together. Focus on just a few to get started. If practical, provide opportunities for staff members to observe each other and collect evidence on ways to shift the role students play in their own learning.

5. Engage your staff in a discussion regarding current practices that may undermine efforts to build learning capacity, ownership, and independence. What needs to be changed or left behind to make room for new learner-centered practices to take root?

4

The Five Key Instructional Shifts
of Personalized Learning

Last semester, I began to incorporate learner voice and choice into assessments. Students are now choosing when to do certain types of assessments and then design their own. I had a student last semester who struggled through Spanish 3, and I worried that I was giving him too much choice—that he was getting lost in all the decision making surrounding his assessments. At the end of the term, as he was handing in his last assessment, he opened up about how much he had enjoyed this form of assessment. He said that in past language classes he felt that he would cram for an exam, partially learn the material, regurgitate it on the exam, and then promptly forget it. He said that this form of assessment (performance assessment)—along with the fact that he could design his own, choosing how to demonstrate his knowledge—made him constantly reuse information. For the first time, he actually felt like he understood what he had learned and could remember the information! At that moment I felt like I was really on the right path.

—Danielle Chaussee, Spanish teacher, Oconomowoc
High School, Oconomowoc, Wisconsin

One of the aspects of personalized learning that is most exciting to me as an educator is the shift from viewing education as an institution to looking at it as a process, the cultivation of a life-long approach to learning that isn't bound by clocks or walls. This shared philosophical shift by our staff has helped us on our journey. We view obstacles to our work as speed bumps rather than insurmountable blockades.

—Randy Daul, principal, Asa Clark Middle School,
Pewaukee, Wisconsin

Mary Connor, a sixth-year teacher, has come to you for help. Though she is an excellent, committed professional, she is frustrated because, despite her best instructional efforts, too many of her students are not committed to learning what she has planned for them. She also finds that too many of them either are unable to work at a pace that she believes is necessary to keep them on track to finish by the end of the year or, conversely, already understand what she is planning to teach them and thus become easily bored.

Ms. Connor reports that she is working as hard as she can, but her efforts are not generating the quality and consistency of results that she thought would be possible at her level of experience and with the amount of professional development around classroom management, curriculum, assessment, and instructional strategies in which she has engaged. She wants to know what else she can do to help all of her students find success. She has contemplated referring struggling students to other specialists and programs. In some extreme cases she actually has made referrals, but she feels responsible for the learning of her students, and sending them to others feels like an admission that she is incapable of meeting their needs. She would like to know what else she might do to engage her students, meet their specific needs, and position them to work with her to build their learning rather than thinking of instruction as something that is done "to" them. You recall having had many of the same feelings as Ms. Connor during the years you spent in the classroom and are tempted to empathize without offering any real answers, but you also want to give some thought to how she might reposition her teaching and her learners in ways that would lead to better results for everyone.

Obviously, Ms. Connor is facing a common dilemma. The traditional design of schools and classes was not intended to help all or even nearly all students to find academic success; students were expected to proceed through the same lessons at the same pace regardless of readiness, interest, aspiration, or background knowledge. This model works when we only need *some* students to do well in school, but it is unsuited to the present day, when we want virtually all learners to achieve at high levels.

In this chapter, we explore five key shifts in instructional practice that significantly increase the probability of learning success for all students while also nurturing learner engagement, ownership, and persistence. We encourage you to reflect on these shifts and consider how they might help teachers in your school facing the same dilemmas as Ms. Connor. Perhaps you can lead a study group of a few teachers to explore, employ, and perfect these shifts before sharing with the rest of the faculty.

Shift 1: Instruction Focused on Curriculum, Pacing, and Presentation → Instruction Focused on Content, Competencies, and Actual Learning from the Students' Perspective

We have traditionally thought of instruction as a matter of identifying the aspects of the curriculum to be presented, determining the pace at which they will be taught, and planning how they will be introduced—all based on factors that may or may not reflect the perspectives and readiness of learners. The first shift asks teachers to start the process of designing instruction with the learner—rather than the curriculum, pacing guide, or teachers' instructional preferences—foremost in mind. The goal is to focus on how best to nurture student learning rather than how best to deliver instruction.

This shift does not imply that teachers should ignore the curriculum, completely reject pacing issues, or give no thought to lesson planning, but rather that they should begin their work by focusing on where learners currently are and building from there to actions that will increase the likelihood that students actually learn and do well in the classroom.

Obviously, this shift requires teachers to understand what their students already know, what they're ready to learn, and what they are likely to find compelling enough to pursue. As teachers make the shift, their students are likely to become progressively more open about sharing their background knowledge and learning preferences.

To help teachers make this shift, coach them to consider the following planning-related questions:

- **Do my students see the relevance and value of what we want them learn?** When students see that what teachers are asking them to learn has value for them beyond the classroom, their perspectives on learning start to change. Teachers might engage learners in discussions about the relevance of their learning to their lives outside school, how it can move them closer to meeting life goals, and how it can prepare them for further learning about what is particularly important to them.
- **Are the competencies clear and compelling?** Teachers may not think much about being transparent with students about

the competencies they are being asked to develop. Yet we know that when students have a clear idea of what they are expected to learn and what success looks like, when competencies are presented in student-friendly language, and when students can see why what they're learning might be compelling to them, they are more likely to commit to their learning and to persist in the face of challenges.

- **What skills, strategies, and other resources are necessary for students to experience success?** Asking students to learn new skills or concepts without considering whether they have the necessary background knowledge and competencies to do so is unfair, yet many students find themselves in this predicament frequently throughout their academic careers. Creating a level playing field for learners requires teachers to take the time to be clear with students about what they will need to be successful.

- **How do I ensure balance between what students are ready to learn and the standards they are expected to master?** Many educators assume that their first responsibility is to the standards or curriculum, when in fact these elements are of little value if students do not or cannot master them. The most important element is student learning, and educators need to focus their attention on ensuring that it occurs before anything else. Once learner readiness is clear, standards and content can be matched and positioned for learning.

- **How am I going to measure learning outcomes?** Most learning can be measured in more than one way, which allows teachers to design assessment activities that are both aligned to the intended learning and responsive to the preferences and capacities of learners. When teachers let students know how their learning will be measured at the beginning of a lesson or ask them to help define assessment activities, students are more motivated to learn.

Shift 2: Learning on Demand →
Instruction on Demand

In a traditional education system, teachers decide what, when, and where students are going to learn; how much time they have to learn it; and whether or not they've learned it. They make most of the decisions affecting student learning and then expect learners to be ready on demand at the appointed time and place to do what they're told to do. The second shift asks educators to offer students some voice in and ownership of their learning and to begin where students currently are and work from there. Ask teachers to consider the following questions to help them focus their attention and energy on responding to learners' needs:

- **How can I create flexibility in content, skill, and knowledge development in order to meet students where they are and spark their desire to learn?** Teachers need to focus on making curriculum and learning expectations suit the students rather than the reverse.
- **What information do I need to have in order to understand what instruction my students need?** This is where having an up-to-date learner profile in place can be most helpful. Knowing where learners are in their learning and what approach is likely to be most successful for them makes answering this question much easier. Of course, teachers can and should ask learners to help guide instructional efforts as well.
- **What resources can I provide to support students' learning paths?** There may be more resources available to teachers than they initially might think. In addition to providing direct instruction, teachers can encourage their students to tap one another's skills and knowledge, access online resources, and meet with community members to deepen their understanding and apply new learning in ways that are both practical and unique to each individual learner.

- **Based on what I know about my individual students, what actions can I take to increase their learning success?** It may be necessary for teachers to adjust their approaches to backfill learning for some students so that success is a realistic option for them. At the same time, teachers should ensure that students who already possess all the necessary background knowledge and may already know much of what they're being asked to learn are appropriately challenged and continue to learn.

- **What instruction will my students need to support the next stage of learning?** Teachers' attention to student learning needs to go beyond the present and extend to what comes next. Coaching and nurturing a broader skill set, introducing key relationships and connections, and providing embellished background information can all add value to learning if introduced at the right time and in the right way for each student. Rather than focus narrowly on success today, teachers should preview what lies ahead so that students can see the value of their current efforts.

Shift 3: Learning Driven by General Assumptions and Vague Reasons → Learning Driven by Clear Purpose

Most of us have had the experience as students of asking why we had to learn something only to be told that we would need it next year, or in high school, or in college, or after graduation. Unfortunately, such vague, answers are not particularly effective either for clarifying purpose or for convincing students that what they're learning is important. Similarly, responding that the new learning will be needed to perform well on an upcoming test invites learners to absorb what is needed for the test and then quickly forget it, assuming the information will no longer be useful. When the purpose for learning is clear, compelling, and specific, students are more likely to engage in the efforts necessary to absorb what they are taught and retain what they learn.

This shift is about focusing the purpose of learning to build relevance and concentrate student attention. Teachers need to help students understand how what they're asked to learn will make their lives better today rather than far in the future, providing specific and useful examples when possible. One way of thinking of this shift is as one from asking students to learn "just in case" to assuring them that they're learning "just in time." Here are some questions teachers can consider regarding this shift:

- **How clear am I making the purpose and utility of what students are learning?** If teachers are not clear about the purpose of learning, it seems unrealistic to expect most students to discover it on their own. If our descriptions are vague, we can expect students to respond by being unfocused in their efforts or retaining what they learn only until they've been assessed on it.
- **How can I convey the purpose of learning in ways that make sense to students?** To be highly effective, teachers need to know their students well and be willing to ask them for more information when necessary to serve their learning needs. Some purposes will be obvious and easy to convey, especially if students routinely set personal learning goals and develop action plans for achieving them. For these students, occasional reminders are all that's necessary. For others, teachers may need to make the purpose clear early on and be very specific about it.
- **How can I help students discover the purpose of their learning by engaging them in exploration, discussion, or investigation?** When students are asked to actively participate in discovering and defining the purpose of their learning, their sense of ownership for their work grows, their persistence increases, and their outcomes generally improve.

This is particularly true for students engaged in project- and problem-based learning activities, as a clear purpose helps students to narrow the scope of their attention and work. Engaging students in the process of discovering purpose allows them to clearly see the "why" of their learning.

- **What applications of the learning will enrich students' lives, increase their power, or move them closer to a goal?** This question goes beyond the "why" of learning to address its specific benefits to students, such as the opening up of opportunities that hadn't been available to them before. Benefits will be especially appealing to students if they dovetail with goals to which they've already committed. Teachers should also help students to understand that in today's world, the very skill of learning itself gives us greater power in the world around us. Increasing personal power can be a strong motivator.

- **What will I do if I can't convince students of the purpose or value of the learning?** Obviously, it can be a challenge to engage learners when we can't give them a good reason to learn. Unfortunately, many educators simply assume that students won't ever be able see the purpose of their learning, so they don't even try to help them discover it. This approach prevents students from discovering the value of learning for intrinsic rather than extrinsic reasons.

  If an immediate purpose is not available, teachers should shift attention to the value of gaining a new skill or having access to useful information. Students who can see and experience the *value* of learning are typically willing to engage in their work without necessarily being clear on its purpose, confident that it will reveal itself in time. It is only when students can see neither the value nor the purpose of learning despite teachers' best efforts that extrinsic rewards should be relied upon, and then only for the short term, lest students become overly reliant on them and distracted from the value of learning.

- **What will I do if *I* can't see the purpose or value of the learning?** Occasionally, teachers may themselves struggle to see the purpose of what they're asked to teach. When this happens, simply deciding not to teach the material is typically not a wise decision. Rather, teachers should take the opportunity to explore the material and learn from others—by accessing professional development networks online, for example, or consulting colleagues. Simply posing a question can provide a wealth of insights and opinions. Teachers fortunate enough to work with a curriculum coordinator might find that he or she is a valuable resource, too; in fact, conversations about the purpose and value of learning can be helpful during the curriculum review processes, highlighting as they do the "why" rather than just the "what." It may be that there is no compelling purpose or that the original purpose is no longer relevant and we should remove the learning from our expectations, but this should be the last option we consider, not the first.

Shift 4: Focusing on Content Accumulation → Building Learning Capacity

Historically, schools have disproportionately focused instruction and assessment on students' accumulation of content and ability to repeat back what they've learned. In a relatively slow-changing world, this approach made some sense; most facts remained true for a long time. Today, the world is changing at a pace that makes rote memorization of a lot of content impractical. Further, most of us now carry with us technology that makes accessing simple facts easy and immediate. For these reasons, it makes sense for teachers to focus on helping students to develop an understanding of systems, relationships, concepts, strategies, and processes related to their learning.

As Eric Hoffer puts it, "In a world of change, learners inherit the earth, while the learned find themselves perfectly suited for a world that no longer exists." Our focus must be on developing the skills, strategies, habits, and tools necessary for students to learn rather than asking them to carry isolated facts in their minds. Certainly, content remains important, but mostly when considered in the context of important concepts and skills. To that end, teachers can consider the following questions:

- **What skills and background knowledge do students need to support upcoming learning tasks?** Students who lack the necessary prerequisites for learning success are more likely to lose their focus, engage in off-task behaviors, and otherwise resist instruction. Knowing what students will need and ensuring that they have the necessary tools to succeed in learning is crucial.
- **How will the content that students are exposed to help them to learn more effectively?** Teachers should avoid asking learners to master content that will not help them to grow their learning capacity. They need to identify content that is engaging to students and furthers their current learning, with more challenging content as students advance.
- **How am I helping students to become more powerful learners?** When teachers start thinking of their purpose as developing *powerful learners* rather than simply *proficient students,* they focus on content and skills that learners can leverage for long-term success, not simply for doing well on classroom and other assessments. Traditional assessments continue to play a role, but primarily in support of larger learning goals and capacity development.
- **How will I measure student learning capacity?** Tools such as rubrics, reflection protocols, and behavioral checklists can be effective for measuring the learning capacity of students. Efficacy, ownership, learning independence, persistence,

and use of learning strategies are all appropriate assessment criteria and can be relatively easy to observe in action and through self-reports (if not always suitable for capturing in a five-question quiz). The secret is to pay more attention to students' patterns of behavior when learning rather than focus on isolated and out-of-context assessments.

- **How will I help students apply their growing learning capacity to the next learning challenge?** Students are more likely to retain new knowledge when teachers give them frequent and meaningful opportunities to use it. In doing so, teachers also reinforce the purpose and value of the learning at hand.

Shift 5: Ensuring Access → Ensuring Success

For decades, educators have focused on ensuring that students have access to a wide variety of learning opportunities, environments, and supports. This attention is important and it needs to continue, but it's not enough. If we allow ourselves to be satisfied with providing access alone, we deny our students the experience of a more intimate and productive relationship with their learning—one that can assure their success, both now and in the future.

Though the shift from ensuring access to ensuring success is more nuanced than the other shifts discussed in this chapter, it is no less important. Here are some questions teachers can ask themselves:

- **What opportunities and supports are necessary for learning success?** Teachers must recognize the importance of moving beyond providing basic access; what happens as a result of the access is more important that the access itself. The challenge is to make any adjustments to instruction necessary to guarantee opportunities and supports that position learners to find success.

- **Do learners have access to the opportunities and supports they need to achieve success?** Teachers must challenge themselves to provide learners with the necessary tools, the optimal environment, and sufficient time to make learning possible, but they must also keep in mind that these alone are insufficient to ensure the learning success of all students.

- **How will I know when learners are struggling so that I can intervene early?** We know that the earlier teachers intervene when learners struggle, the more likely it is that the interventions will succeed. We also know that early interventions are less expensive and typically require less time than ones that come later, when learners have become increasingly disengaged. The foundation for successful intervention is the relationship between learners and educators. Ongoing, open communication can reduce the risk that learning struggles will go unnoticed. Robust systems of data collection and analysis can also help teachers in their efforts to know when intervention is needed. One key to success is regular monitoring of learning progress.

- **What intervention strategies will I employ when learners encounter barriers to learning?** There's an old saying: "When your only tool is a hammer, every problem looks like a nail." Teachers need to have as wide an array of intervention strategies available to them as possible. If they find that they don't have effective options at hand to address a particular challenge, leaders need to be ready to provide them with the support they need to expand their repertoires.

- **What learning supports are available to me to help struggling learners?** Obviously, there will be times when students require supports that teachers alone can't provide. It is vital, then, that teachers have access to a wide variety of additional resources they in turn can offer to learners. If teachers can't locate necessary resources, leaders need to help them to do so.

ACTIVITY

Student Positioning Related to Learning

Time: 60 to 90 minutes

Type: Reflective

Who: Teams of educators

Difficulty: 3 out of 5

This gets you: In the learner's mindset to reflect on learner-centered strategies.

Keep in mind: You may want to revisit this activity later on in the design process as well. At this stage, the exercise can help educators understand the shift in the value proposition we present to learners that is inherent in personalized learning.

Ask teachers to place themselves in the position of students who are resistant to learning, compliant with directions, and committed to success. For each category in the following chart, ask them to describe the attributes for the three types of learners.

Student Positioning Related to Learning

	Types of Learners		
	Resistant	Compliant	Committed
Perceptions about learning			
Behaviors when learning			
Relationships with others related to learning			
Goals related to learning			

Next, ask teachers to use the insights they've gained from filling out the chart to complete the one on the next page—this time from their own perspectives as educators—by listing the strategies that they might adopt for each category to support the three types of learners.

Student Positioning Related to Learning: High-Leverage Teacher Strategies

	Types of Learners		
	Resistant	Compliant	Committed
Perceptions about learning			
Behaviors when learning			
Relationships with others related to learning			
Goals related to learning			

Reflection Questions

1. Think back to Ms. Connor at the beginning of this chapter. What was missing in her approach that may have led to student coasting, boredom, and disruption?
2. How have you provided support to teachers like Ms. Connor in the past? How might your approach change as a result of what you read in this chapter?
3. How might looking at learning content and competencies through the eyes of students lead to new insights when designing lessons?
4. How much emphasis do teachers in your school place on students understanding and valuing the purpose of what they are learning? What examples can you offer?
5. How might a shift from focusing on student access to learning opportunities to ensuring successful learning change the processes, supports, and outcomes students in your school experience?

Actions You Can Take

1. Hold a focus group with a diverse group of staff members to discuss the implications of the five instructional shifts discussed in this chapter. Ask them the following questions: What evidence is there that these shifts have already occurred at our school? Where are opportunities available to implement the shifts? Which shifts would make the greatest difference to student success?
2. Convene a series of focus groups made up of diverse learners. Frame four to six questions based on the five shifts and invite learners to share their experiences with each shift. To what extent do students find instruction to be calibrated to meet their individual learning needs and readiness levels? Do they believe they are focusing on building important

life skills, or do they feel that they spend most of their time memorizing decontextualized facts? Do they see purpose in what they are learning? Summarize your findings for staff and schedule a meeting for discussion and analysis. Compare and contrast learner and educator perspectives on the five shifts.

3. Conduct an inventory of strategies that teachers at your school are already using to help learners understand and experience the purpose of their learning. Generate a list of examples and practices to share and invite others to add to it.

4. Ask staff members to think of the expectations and processes that they might need to abandon to shift their focus from content accumulation to building learning capacity. Then, ask them to identify new expectations and processes better aligned to personalized learning.

5. Spend time by yourself considering how the experiences of learners in your school will change if the five shifts discussed in this chapter are implemented. What evidence will you need to assess whether or not the shifts have been successful?

5

Building Educator Capacity: Personalized Professional Development

As our staff has become more enlightened and sophisticated in their understanding of personalized learning, they have more and more questioned existing practices that do not support their own or their students' growth in a personalized manner. From professional development to operational items such as schedules, staff feel more empowered as a result of our journey. A strong focus on distributive leadership philosophies and tight-loose management techniques has been necessary to provide a collaborative and aligned approach to our growth. The excitement that surrounds transforming teaching and learning practices must be in balance with the needs of the organization and its stakeholders.

—Randy Daul, principal, Asa Clark Middle School, Pewaukee, Wisconsin

It is Monday morning in mid-October. Every educator in Middle Valley School is gathered in the lobby outside the cafeteria enjoying coffee, juice, and pastries and visiting with colleagues. Then

comes the announcement: everyone is to gather inside for the day's professional development session. Today's speaker will address the topic of giving and grading good homework.

Jane, a kindergarten teacher, is struggling to make a connection, as she rarely gives homework to her students. Bill, the physical education teacher, thinks about homework in terms of healthy activities that he wants his students to engage in but sees little value in assessing what they do. Mary, a 5th grade teacher, has read several recent studies showing that homework generates little learning value and can exaggerate existing inequities among students with different levels of home support and background knowledge; she wonders if there will be an opportunity to discuss whether homework should ever be assigned. John, a new teacher who has trouble getting his students to complete their homework, is excited to hear and apply what he will learn today.

The morning unfolds in a manner familiar to most educators. After multiple announcements, the presenter is introduced as an expert who has developed a number of techniques for assigning and grading homework. He discusses his experience with homework from when he used to teach, including a number of humorous stories describing excuses students gave him about why they did not complete their homework or how it was destroyed before they could turn it in. He argues that homework is a good way to teach discipline and reinforce what is taught during daily lessons, but cautions that assignments should be short so students will complete them. He discusses five techniques for quickly reviewing and assigning scores to completed homework and observes that homework can be a way to involve parents in their children's learning (unless they do it for their children, of course). The session concludes with polite applause but with no specific expectation that anyone will apply what has been presented or significant discussion of how it might address the specific issues and concerns of staff members.

Joe, the principal, returns to his office later in the day to spend a few minutes reviewing evaluations of the day's session from his teachers. With each completed form he reads, he becomes more disappointed. Teachers complained that the topic of the presentation was irrelevant to their practice and that the issue of whether or not homework was even necessary went unaddressed. Only a few of the teachers found the session valuable and expressed any eagerness to apply what they had learned from it.

Each of us probably has experienced days not unlike the one described above. It's easy to understand why many educators do not see the value of this type of professional development (PD) and may even dread having to engage in it. If we want educators to value personalized learning experiences for students, they must experience the benefits of it in their *own* learning. And yet, time and again, we persist in asking teachers to engage in PD that is irrelevant to their practice. Too often, these learning opportunities are of a one-size-fits-all nature and may not even apply to all teachers. In addition, sessions tend to be scheduled to fit breaks in the school calendar rather than offered when they are most needed and will serve a specific and immediate purpose.

Research on the effectiveness of traditional PD approaches has documented their shortcomings for decades (Darling-Hammond, Chung Wel, Andree, Richardson, & Orphanos, 2009). If we hope to change professional practices, we must offer teachers (and help them to identify and develop) professional learning experiences that are timely, customized to their learning needs and readiness levels, and available in a variety of formats (e.g., large group, independent, online).

The principles that underlie effective learning are the same for educators as they are for students. In fact, the set of personalized learning elements discussed in Chapter 2 is also applicable to adult learning opportunities. Professional learning experiences should focus on building efficacy and ownership among educators, offer voice and choice, meet educators where they are, and address their specific needs in the context of a shared vision. The long-term goal of all learning opportunities should be to support educators in developing the skills necessary to become self-directed professionals.

Unfortunately, many school leaders are skeptical about the efficacy of a personalized approach to professional learning, fearing that teachers won't use their time wisely, or that if they cede too much control teachers won't make responsible choices and chaos will result. Of course, these are the same fears that teachers express when implementing personalized learning in their classroom, and evidence shows that students respond in amazingly positive ways. Leaders cannot expect teachers to value and offer personalized experiences to learners if they are not willing to provide them with the same types of opportunities.

Just as teachers must take the first steps to change the learning environment for their students, school leaders must offer flexibility and control to teachers while establishing a clear purpose for learning, aligning work to standards and expectations, and providing the support necessary for a transition to personalized professional learning. If leaders are unwilling to provide this type of learning environments for adults, they cannot expect a robust implementation of personalized learning at the classrooms level.

Returning to the scenario at the start of this chapter, let's imagine what a personalized vision of professional learning might look like. The morning might start in much the same way, with educators sharing refreshments and pleasantries—but in this case the conversations also extend to discussion about where they're each focusing their learning energies that day in light of current professional goals, action research projects, and other learning priorities:

- One group of colleagues meets to discuss how to help low-confidence learners take greater risks, sharing their struggles and triumphs as they learn from each other. They also hold a video conference with an expert from another state or country who can address their specific issues. At the end of their meeting, the teachers each commit to try a particular strategy and share results the next time the group meets.
- Another group reviews data on the responses of students with different learner profiles to learning goals and action plans. They look for patterns and trends that suggest the need for a wider array of conferencing strategies and follow-up activities to ensure that students take responsibility for their learning. As the day unfolds, these teachers identify promising approaches to try with their students and agree to report back when the group reconvenes.
- Another group divides its time between individual activities and group debriefing in a blended-learning course on effective project-based learning practices. After completing self-assessments of their personalization strategies and tools, some members of this group recognize that they need to expand the number and scope of strategies in their personalization "tool-boxes" to better meet the needs of diverse learners.
- Teachers in another group spend part of their day exploring and sharing strategies for seeing learning from the students' perspectives. They challenge themselves to use this information to design learning activities that will tap the interests and match the readiness levels of all learners. In addition to

sharing strategies, these teachers explore ways to use what they learn about student readiness to help students understand and meet standards.

• Still another group explores the role of homework in personalized instruction, starting with an overview of what each of the group members understands about it, what the research says about its effectiveness, and how teachers might adjust their practices to match the needs of all learners. This group commits to sharing its findings with other educators through a combination of short videos and a series of blogs.

Predictably, evaluation results for teachers in our updated scenario are markedly different from those in the example at the start of this chapter and include commitments to specific actions for improving practice and contributing to shared professional learning. At the end of the day, the principal spends some time reviewing what each group has achieved and updating the school's skills and capacity profile, which includes educators' growing skillsets, research findings, and professional learning resources from which all staff can benefit.

Not only does a personalized approach to professional learning give educators firsthand experience with personalization so that they can understand how it might affect students, but it also allows them to build their capacity to support one another as well as learners in the classroom. A fully personalized school culture promises to offer the stimulation, nurturing, mutual support, and professional identity that so many teachers seek, but so few find, in their professional lives.

As with personalized learning for students, we need to begin the process of personalizing professional learning with individual learners in mind. Whereas some educators will be reluctant to make the shift and will need more time, examples, and support than their peers, others will find the changes refreshing and move quickly to embrace them.

Individual Professional Learning Profiles

Educators in a personalized ecosystem typically have individual professional learning profiles that include the following elements:

- Self-assessments and other measures of current skills
- Descriptions of professional learning goals and personal learning paths
- An ongoing action research project in an area of interest or expertise or an area of struggle
- A portfolio or other representation of progress toward achievement of key goals and evidence of learning
- A description of how achieving professional learning goals will benefit students, teachers, and the school as a whole
- Personal reflections about professional learning experiences that shaped educators' insights, philosophies, and professional identities

When developing profiles, the key is to focus on elements that will provide the greatest insights and direction for continued learning and not become distracted by "nice-to-have" items that don't really address staff needs.

The goals and plans included in professional learner profiles should serve as the starting points for professional learning activities. It can be tempting for leaders to design a professional learning program for staff based on the information from their profiles, but doing so risks taking away the ownership, commitment, and sense of responsibility that educators need to experience. A better option is to hold a "generating session" with all staff to collect professional learning ideas during which leaders share models and approaches that other schools have used to broaden the discussion. Then, leaders convene a smaller group to take promising ideas and create a variety of options to support flexible paths for individuals and groups to consider as they reflect on their goals and learning plans. Leaders must leave open the possibility for additional ideas that staff might want to try. Essentially, leaders need to scaffold the learning of staff rather than attempt to confine or overstructure their experiences. Multiple iterations of any approach will be necessary to get the support structure right, and even then it will need frequent tweaking.

Measuring the Effects of Professional Learning

Traditionally, we have measured professional development based on attendance at sessions, assessment questions to determine levels of knowledge acquisition, and staff self-reflections. Although these data are helpful, they do little to measure the degree to which new learning affects teacher practice. A better way to do so is to provide teachers with opportunities to demonstrate new knowledge and skills. Borrowing from the array of assessment strategies that they use with students, teachers might teach others what they have learned; demonstrate new learning to an audience of students, other educators, or experts; write blog posts and articles; or develop short videos to show what they've learned. Approaches such as these can impart the richness of professional learning while informing the practice of colleagues.

Leaders can also provide educators with the option of creating artifacts showing how they've applied new learning. And, of course, depending on the specific learning being assessed, leaders might consider observations and relevant data on how students are responding to changes in teachers' instruction to understand what is having an effect and where additional learning and practice are necessary.

Once leaders have a basic idea in place of what teachers' learning plans should look like, they can add dimensions and tools of support. One good option is to pair teachers with colleagues whom they respect and who are committed to helping them grow in their learning. Often, the questions colleagues ask can shed light on teachers' thinking, open new avenues for exploration, and point them to new tools and techniques as they continue to evolve in their practice.

Online communities allow educators to connect regularly and share ideas, questions, and resources, including tools to support instructional activities, give learners greater independence, or organize information in real time. Teachers involved in online learning can engage in synchronous and asynchronous learning activities without having to waste time looking for and traveling to an adequate physical space. Our work with school districts is filled with examples of educators who connect with each other and share what they are learning and developing online. For example, the technology director at one of our urban school districts once posted online asking for help developing learner profiles and goal sheets for early learners. Among the dozens of colleagues who responded, one was a kindergarten teacher from a rural community who shared her entire resource file with him. Not only did this approach yield extraordinary feedback, it was inexpensive and saved hours of work.

ACTIVITY

Identifying Professional Development Needs

Time: 30 to 60 minutes

Type: Reflective

Who: 5 or more staff, comprehensive implementation team

Difficulty: 3 out of 5

This gets you: To identify the possible professional learning needs of staff early on. Think broadly: what additional knowledge and skills will educators need to implement a full-scale personalization model in your school?

Keep in mind: Educators' professional learning needs will expand as personalization expands and more teachers become involved.

Compile a list of immediate needs that must be addressed before the personalized professional learning process gets underway. We suggest you start by holding conversations with the initial group of educators who will be piloting the program. (Don't just guess what their needs are—ask!) Then, compile two more lists: one of short-term needs that must be addressed before the end of the semester or year and one of long-term needs that must be addressed by next year or before expanding the program further.

Reflection Questions

1. To what extent do the professional learning opportunities your educators experience reflect and respond to their specific, individual learning needs?
2. What flexibility do you have within your school to redesign professional learning processes so that they reflect the types of learning experiences you want educators to offer to their students?
3. Who within your school or school district might be best positioned and willing to help you with this work?
4. What examples of personalized professional learning already exist for your staff that you can build upon to construct a more comprehensive model?
5. How might you leverage available technology to change and expand the professional learning options available to your staff?

Actions You Can Take

1. Set aside time at a staff meeting to ask educators to reflect on their most powerful professional learning experiences. Follow up by asking them to share in groups what it was that made their experiences so powerful. Next, ask the members of each group to identify common characteristics of their experiences and report out to the whole group. Listen and note what is shared. You likely will hear about experiences that were timely, addressed specific learning needs and readiness levels, allowed some degree of ownership, and offered opportunities for immediate application of new learning. This activity can be a starting point for the journey to redesign professional learning in your school.

2. Identify a key group of educators within your school or district to help you design an initial professional learning cycle that is driven by staff needs and readiness rather than the schedule. To the extent possible, structure the learning cycle to provide flexibility for educators to participate in designing their learning activities. Encourage staff to collaborate in planning and carrying out the cycle. Ask that each activity be aligned to a learning goal and require evidence of learning, but allow staff to decide how to develop the learning. Use this experience to demonstrate the potential of personalization to increase engagement, build professional learning, and respond to individual and shared learning needs. Not everything will go perfectly, so be ready to listen and learn.

3. Draw insights from discussions with staff about their learning preferences, and offer suggestions to help them to build professional learner profiles. Consider the skills educators will need to support personalized learning for students, and have them develop an inventory of their current skill set. (See Appendix C for an example of an educator skill set.)

You can add other inventories and assessments to each profile, but be careful at this point to include only information that the teacher can act upon immediately. Anything else can become a distraction.

4. Ask members of your staff to use their learner profiles, the standards they are working with students to achieve, and any other immediately relevant goals and challenges to create a limited set of professional learning goals. At the start of the personalization process, this list of goals should include no more than three items; a single compelling and challenging goal might be enough, depending on its scope and potential impact. Next, ask teachers to develop an action plan for achieving each goal. The plan should include the resources necessary to develop learning activities, including any that they will have to find outside school, and should specify methods of assessing and demonstrating progress. Be aware that developing an action plan may take some time, but that without experiencing the process themselves, teachers will struggle to support it properly with their learners.

5. As the personalized professional learning process expands, look for ways to create additional supports. For example, peer coaches can provide mutual accountability and help teachers to devise new and better approaches. Consider creating an online community that staff can use to share ideas and develop a shared sense of ownership. Encourage staff to expand their personal learning networks beyond the school and district.

6

Secrets to Scaling and Sustaining Transformation

Scaling personalized learning is a challenge—a messy one! You are constantly confronted by fixed mindsets and entrenched structures and practices. Through the ups and downs, the steps forward and backward, it is critical to maintain the philosophical mindset that personalizing education through learner-centered experiences is in the best interest of each child. Although it is important for there to be a level of urgency to our work, there is also a need for a high degree of patience—this isn't work that is done overnight or in a single school year. We are on a journey to a destination that isn't yet defined, so enjoy the process. As we emphasize to our students that education isn't simply a product, we sometimes need to remind ourselves that it isn't about the destination. We are not just helping children grow—we are also growing ourselves as educators.

—Randy Daul, principal, Asa Clark Middle School, Pewaukee, Wisconsin

The Institute for Personalized Learning transformed my view of personalized learning through professional development, site visits, and collaboration. I was able to fully understand the power of providing students with customized learning paths so that they had a voice in what they would learn and how they would demonstrate their learning. This truly empowered and engaged our kindergarten learners. What I learned not only allowed me to grow as an educator, but also provided a model to positively affect all students at our school. For example, our 4th grade and kindergarten teams have collaborated together to implement a learning lab into our daily routine. The lab is a time when all students are given opportunities to work on personal learning goals, engage in hands-on learning, and utilize technology. We are excited for the upcoming school year because all grade-level teams will be implementing the learning lab into their daily routines.

—Michele Baumann, teacher, Elmbrook School
District, Wisconsin

For the past several years, a team of teachers in the school where John is principal has led an innovative school-within-a-school program using project-based learning known as "the Neighborhood." Students who were a part of the program loved the experience and were committed to their involvement. Test scores were strong, so the district office was willing to continue supporting the program even though it cost a little more than traditional classroom instruction. Teachers in the Neighborhood were dedicated to their students and the success of the program. Some other teachers on the staff occasionally complained that these teachers had more flexible schedules than they did, but there was no significant or sustained resistance to the program.

Everything seemed fine until more parents than could be accommodated in the program began to ask that their children be included. Then, parents from other schools began asking for a similar program for their children. Unfortunately, other staff members at John's school were not interested in joining or expanding the program. John was faced with telling parents that the best he could do was either to place their children on a waiting list or to assign teachers to the program who were not committed to its philosophy and did not understand the value of the approach.

Just as John was about to decide, two key staff members involved with the Neighborhood were recruited by another school district. The remaining team members decided that, rather than to try to recompose the team with new members, they would return to traditional classroom assignments and attempt to integrate project-based learning where they could.

John now is left with no program. He is reflecting on what went wrong. Why didn't the program grow? It was obviously working for students. Did he miss something along the way? Were there steps he could have taken from the beginning that might have sustained and grown the program? Was there a leadership issue? Was something wrong with the culture of the school? Maybe it's too late for the Neighborhood, but John wants to learn what went wrong before encouraging staff to engage in another innovative program.

The Challenge of Scaling

Scaling innovation in education is a special challenge due in part to the way in which it typically is approached. Too often, pockets of innovation depend excessively on a single person or small group of people to implement and sustain the work. Frequently, there is an absence of a clear, documented theory of action. At other times, there is a lack of understanding among staff regarding the core elements and factors driving the innovation. Also common is the absence of a plan for scaling from the time of original design. Consequently, preparations and resources to make scaling possible are not available.

Although little research is available to guide scaling innovation in education, the KnowledgeWorks Foundation recently identified 10 conditions that are necessary for scaling efforts to succeed (Williams, Moyer, & Jenkins, 2014):

1. Curriculum aligned to the vision for teaching and learning
2. Instructional practices focused on teaching students how to learn, shifting from teacher-led to student-led while maintaining rigor and relevance
3. A comprehensive assessment system including formative, interim, and summative assessments that feature a variety of performance portfolio and capstone projects and processes
4. Learning environments that are flexible, inclusive, equitable, and trust based
5. Student supports and interventions that are informed by formative assessments and frequent feedback to learners
6. Professional development that fosters a culture of collaboration and continuous improvement
7. Leadership development available at the classroom, school, and district levels
8. Technology policies that support ubiquitous and safe access to the Internet
9. Comprehensive data systems to support learning management, assessment activities, and student information
10. Partnerships with business, community, and higher education constituents

Of course, addressing and sustaining all of these conditions over time is a complex and daunting challenge for any leader. In addition, maintaining momentum in the face of opposing forces generated by the status quo can feel overwhelming. Leaders can face challenges from a variety of sources—from traditional practices that are not aligned to the innovation and processes for allocating resources that are based on contrary operating assumptions to undermining efforts from those who prefer the comfort and predictability of past traditions and fear having to engage in new and unfamiliar practices.

Scouts, Pioneers, Settlers, and Saboteurs

Watching the spread of personalized learning has been an amazing experience. In our work, we have noticed that educators involved in the change process can be grouped into four distinct categories: *scouts, pioneers, settlers,* and *saboteurs.*

Scouts

At the start of the process, a small group of adventuresome and risk-tolerant educators volunteers to explore personalization opportunities for both students and colleagues. We call these educators "scouts." They are willing to implement changes before many aspects of the change initiative are fully comfortable for them. These educators typically ask for limited, direct support and little else beyond basic resources, funding, and flexibility. Independent and innovative, scouts help others to see possibilities and learn key skills and practices and are likely to invite colleagues to join the adventure. Though small in numbers, scouts highlight what is possible if we are willing to take some risks, think differently, and engage in new relationships and strategies.

Pioneers

A second group of educators tends to follow the first wave of innovators once some of the initial implementation is in place. We call this group "pioneers." These educators are willing to take some risks and travel through some yet-to-be-settled territory to learn and test the impact of personalized learning practices and processes with their learners. Pioneers do not necessarily expect to be given detailed directions or to have all of their questions answered in advance, but they do want to know that what they are doing will make a significant difference for their students. They also want basic tools and some experienced guidance to support their work; they understand that mistakes and missteps are part of the learning process for adult learners, too. Pioneers collaborate, share successful practices, and learn from one another's experiences. They also show what will be necessary for success as the next group engages with the process.

Settlers

We call the teachers in this third group "settlers." These educators bring the work to scale and make it the norm. Settlers are committed to doing the best for their students, but they want proven tools and support to develop key skills and practices. They want to be sure that all the pieces of the system fit together, and they want clear and consistent expectations. When settlers engage with the new way of doing things, they also bring the promise of personalized learning within reach of virtually all learners.

Saboteurs

We refer to teachers in the fourth and often unanticipated group as "saboteurs." This group comprises people who do not want to change and do not want the innovation to succeed. Consequently, they work to undermine efforts, sow doubt and uncertainty, and instill fear among colleagues. They typically hide among settlers and ask questions that may sound innocent but are calculated to impede rather than assure. They search for what could go wrong, demand answers that may not yet be available, and often press for accommodations that benefit adults at the expense of students. Saboteurs typically remain quiet while scouts are engaged in exploration and may not surface when pioneers are moving forward. Often they emerge only when they believe they are going to be expected to implement practices associated with the innovation.

Three strategies typically are most effective when dealing with saboteurs. First, leaders need to listen to them carefully and treat them with respect. Settlers often do not realize the motives behind the resistance of saboteurs; if leaders argue with, accuse, or show disrespect toward them, settlers will wonder if their questions will be treated the same way and begin to pull back. Leaders need to engage saboteurs in private whenever possible—their power is diminished if there is no one else present to influence. Leaders must pay attention to what saboteurs have to say and respond with the best information they have. Just because they don't support the innovation doesn't mean that they do not have legitimate questions or concerns. But leaders need to avoid prolonged engagement lest the saboteurs become distractions. The best approach is to minimize saboteurs' influence while supporting and leading others.

Each of the above groups plays a role as we work to make personalized learning a reality, but each requires different types of responses from leaders:

- Scouts need opportunities, flexibility, and support as they try new approaches and develop new understandings.
- Pioneers need assurances that their work is leading to good outcomes for learners, as well as enough support to solidify their practices and see results.
- Settlers need clarity, stability, and direct support to ensure that they are doing what is necessary and expected. For this group, formal professional learning systems need to be in place and standards and accountability expectations need to be in alignment.
- Saboteurs need facts, clarity, and assurance, but leaders must be careful not to overreact or dedicate disproportionate time, energy, and attention to them, especially in front of an audience, as they are committed to spreading fear, instilling doubt, and undermining commitment.

All of these groups need leaders who believe in and advocate for the work ahead, are ready to support their professional journey, and are committed to being learning partners.

Action Network Approach

We discovered early that by working together, sharing our resources and experiences, and learning from each other we could move forward faster, avoid needless missteps and setbacks, provide mutual support (and sometimes protection), and share energy, enthusiasm and courage. Action networks differ from other types of networks (e.g., social, information sharing, career advancement) in that their benefits accrue not only to the members of the network individually, but to the network as a whole.

Networks can be powerful vehicles for creating ideas and mobilizing action. They are voluntary and commitment driven, and they are flexible enough to shift focus and absorb new information much faster and more easily than formal structures. Further, networks can encourage and support divergent ideas, whereas formal structures too often encourage convergent thinking that limits thought and action.

Our thinking about networks has been informed by two strands of research and thought. The first is the idea of "communities of practice" developed by Wenger, McDermott, and Snyder (2002). This approach to collective, collaborative work is based on the following seven principles:

1. Designing for evolution
2. Opening a dialogue between inside and outside perspectives
3. Inviting different levels of participation
4. Developing both public and private community spaces
5. Focusing on value
6. Combining familiarity and excitement
7. Creating a rhythm for the community

The second strand is based on the idea of "network improvement communities" developed by Bryk and Gomez at the Carnegie Foundation (Bryk, Gomez, Grunow, & Lemahieu, 2015). This approach brings together people with a common interest in or concern about a particular challenge and uses a cycle of examination, creation of potential solutions, shared application of potential solutions, data collection, analysis, and application of new learning and insights. This approach, too, is based on a set of core principles:

1. Making the work problem specific and user centered
2. Focusing on variation in performance
3. Seeing the system that produces the current outcomes
4. Improving at scale only what we can measure
5. Engaging in disciplined inquiry to drive improvement
6. Accelerating learning through networked communities

Action Network Norms

Action networks function best when they are supported by a set of explicit, shared norms that clarify how members will work together, ensure focus and accountability, and guide each other as they work on key tasks. The norms of personalized learning action networks include dimensions not necessarily present in other working groups:

The work must be transformational. We have found that unless the work of action networks is aimed at more than incremental adjustments to the current system, it can lead to tinkering with current practices rather than truly redesigning the learning ecosystem.

The network must be grounded in a growing understanding of the power of personalized learning. This norm recognizes that members of the group will be learning together. No one is the ultimate expert; rather, the work is a journey of discovery in which sharing, learning, and applying are key activities.

Scalability and sustainability must be part of the new system design from the beginning. Too often, educators embark on innovation efforts without thinking through how those efforts will be adopted, adapted, expanded, and applied to benefit a growing number of learners, educators, schools, and districts. Grant-funded and pilot programs often fall into this category. Unfortunately, when the funds run out or key people leave, implementation can come to a halt. Additionally, educators risk giving too little thought to whether current and anticipated resources will be enough to move beyond a pilot stage.

Learning gained through the network will be considered open source and shared freely within the network. The idea of sharing within the network can seem foreign and even contrary to the concept of intellectual property. Yet if members don't commit to doing so, the network will be of limited value. The free flow of ideas, strategies, lessons learned, and successes is the lifeblood of effective action networks. This norm must be made clear and enforced early on or the risk of conflict and erosion of trust among members rises.

Tools and instruments will only be modified with the permission of the developer. Though ideas and materials should be shared within the action network, members must pay deference and respect to those who invent, develop, and are willing to share helpful tools or instruments.

Work must hold the promise of raising academic achievement and supporting the learning of all students regardless of current performance levels. This norm addresses the importance of equity in the work of action networks. Educators need to focus on and commit to the learning of *all* learners, not just selected groups. Further, although the goals of personalized learning extend well beyond traditional measures of school success to include what are commonly referred to as 21st century skills, noncognitive skills, or soft skills, if the innovation does not also show results on traditional measures, community permission to continue the work can be withdrawn.

Co-learning among adults and students will be a key component of personalized learning. This norm recognizes that learning should not be confined to students and, indeed, that it can be enhanced when educators engage in it as well.

Building learner, educator, and leadership capacity will be a central focus. Expanding all stakeholders' capacity to learn, teach, and lead is key to the successful transformation of a school's ecosystem. Everyone, students and adults alike, must commit to building their skills, increasing their knowledge, and expanding their experiences if they are to find sustainable success.

Data collection, analysis, application, and management will be a shared responsibility among members of the action network. It is necessary for educators to develop and apply new strategies and approaches, build new frameworks, and provide new learning opportunities for all. To this end, they need to understand what is and isn't working. Collecting, analyzing, and learning from the work is key to stabilizing and sustaining innovation. Unless we systematically use data to guide decisions and allocate effort, progress is likely to be slow and diverted by a variety of forces. As noted earlier, students increasingly need to be trusted to use data to understand, diagnose, and support their learning efforts.

Network members may use different entry points and align their work to preferred areas of focus. This norm recognizes the variety of cultures and contexts within which personalized learning may be implemented. Although the three core elements of the honeycomb model (see p. 37) serve as the innovation platform on which the work is built, network members have a variety of options for moving forward based on their own skills, interests, and preferences.

Our decision to take a regional network approach to the work of personalized learning has helped us to expand from just a few schools to nearly 60 schools involving more than 1,000 teachers and offering tens of thousands of students learning experiences in a learning ecosystem where they are at the center—all in just over five years. Even better, the momentum is continuing to grow and more schools, districts, and educators are joining the work almost every month.

Our experience has shown that a networked approach can overcome many of the barriers to scaling. Action networks can support principals and other leaders as they design, experience, and build personalized learning ecosystems and are much more effective than traditional "affinity" networks.

A Model for Collaboration

We know intuitively that collaboration should make the work of transforming an education ecosystem easier and swifter. However, working with others does not always come naturally to educators who have practiced largely on their own throughout their careers. By understanding the different forms of collaboration and matching collaborative strategies to goals, all educators can benefit from working together to personalize learning.

We have identified five general levels of collaboration, each with its own role and set of benefits. We might think of these levels as forming a pyramid (see Figure 6.1):

1. **Sharing frustrations and emotional release.** The first level, forming the base of our collaboration pyramid because it is so common, involves sharing perceptions and finding emotional relief by complaining to one another, retelling experiences, and sharing opinions about the issues of the day. This level offers practitioners emotional support and a sense of belonging but rarely results in significant new professional learning. In fact, overindulging in this level can actually get in the way of learning and change.

2. **Growing camaraderie and sharing stories.** Moving up the pyramid, we encounter the next level of collaboration. Sharing at this level isn't necessarily focused on finding solutions to challenges, but it can be informative, entertaining, and useful for understanding shared values and ways of thinking. The "war stories" educators share with each other

Figure 6.1
Five Levels of Networking for Collaboration and Engagement

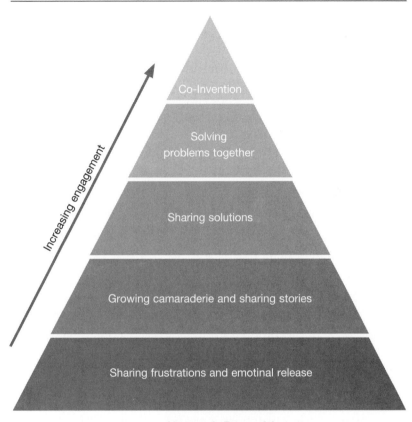

Network Pyramid

can offer context and reinforce thinking about roles, work, expectations, and organizational culture.

3. **Sharing solutions.** The third level of collaboration focuses on identifying and understanding challenges and opportunities related to the change process. Learning at this level of collaboration is intentional, and members of the action network may take turns sharing experiences and insights with the intent of supporting the work of their colleagues.

Insights and potential solutions to problems are grounded in the perceptions and experiences of those who share them, so group members must be careful to translate what they hear to their own contexts.

4. **Solving problems together.** As we approach the top of the pyramid, the collaborative experience becomes increasingly focused. At the fourth level, the entire group is focused on finding solutions to a common problem or challenge. Each member of the network brings his or her best thinking, insights, questions, experience, and expertise to learn to the search for common ideas and solutions. At its best, collaboration at this level can result in outcomes that no single member of the network would be able to achieve alone. Collaboration at this level of sophistication and interdependence offers the potential to improve the learning and effectiveness of all participants.

5. **Co-invention.** At the top of the pyramid is a level of collaboration that typically is rare in education. This highest level of collaboration builds on the work of the fourth level, but it is focused on creating rather than problem solving. At its best, co-invention generates new insights, uncovers new options, and leads to new solutions and approaches from which all participants can benefit and that may have an effect well beyond the work of those directly involved. Although collaboration at this level is more time-consuming and challenging than at the other levels and thus less common, it also holds the promise of a greater return on the effort invested.

As educators engage in the work of redesigning and transforming the learning ecosystems in their schools, all five levels of collaboration can play a role, but it is the top three levels that offer the greatest leverage and most potential to ensure that innovation efforts succeed.

ACTIVITY

Preparing for Expansion

Time: 30 minutes

Type: Reflective

Who: Administrative team

Difficulty: 2 out of 5

This gets you: An understanding of whether others in your school beyond your scouts and pioneers are ready for personalized learning. Are the practices in place and in some areas ready to be 'expanded to new classrooms?

Keep in mind: One critical piece for expansion is ensuring that key leaders are behind the vision of personalized learning. Expansion will be difficult if teachers hear conflicting messages from leadership. Review the key messages and talking points from your communication plan to ensure that leaders are consistent in their messaging. Are you creating space for innovation and rewarding risk?

Rating system values:
1 – Not in place
2 – In process
3 – Substantially in place
4 – In place
5 – Being adjusted or refined

Using the above rating system, consider how each of the statements in the following chart applies to your school.

Leaders have publicly committed to pursue the new vision.	
The school has strategies in place to effectively communicate important milestones and progress to internal audiences, including both proactive and responsive tactics.	
The school has strategies in place to effectively communicate important milestones and progress to external audiences (parents, community leaders, media), including both proactive and responsive tactics.	
Examples of personalized learning efforts are widely communicated within and beyond the organization.	
Examples of personalized learning efforts where early results are showing success are shared throughout and beyond the organization.	
Leaders recognize and reinforce the work of those involved in creating successful examples of personalized learning.	
A robust dialogue regarding personalized learning is under way within the organization.	
A robust dialogue regarding personalized learning is under way within the community.	
Feedback mechanisms for both internal and external audiences are monitored and acted upon.	
Teachers and other staff have received training and possess the capacity to engage in personalized learning strategies and techniques.	

If you indicated mostly 3s and above in the chart, your school is ready to begin the work of shifting toward a fully personalized learning ecosystem! If not, consider engaging in the following actions:

- Provide routine updates to internal stakeholders about progress in implementation.
- Include teacher leaders as you roll the program out to additional staff.
- Continue communicating with external stakeholders, being clear on the why, what, and how of the work and tying the goals of innovation efforts to their particular situations.
- Develop protocols and guidelines to ensure alignment across classrooms and programs.
- Determine a process for assessment and adjustment of the work.

Reflection Questions

1. Why is it so difficult in education to move from good ideas and small pilot programs to full-scale, widespread innovation?
2. Why is it important to take processes and practices that seem to be effective in one context or school and apply them in others as we test and scale innovation? What can we learn from doing this?
3. What about the work of personalization makes it well suited for a collaborative approach?
4. How might action network norms related to personalization differ from other team norms with which you have had experience?
5. What new insights regarding collaboration do the five levels of collaboration discussed in this chapter offer for your work with staff and others?

Actions You Can Take

1. Take some time to think about who among your staff might be natural scouts and pioneers. How can you position and encourage them to test personalized learning practices in your school? What kind of preparation, evidence, and support will your settlers require to move forward? Who might surface as saboteurs, and how can you anticipate and prepare for their questions, objections, and undermining behaviors?

2. Review the list of norms shared in this chapter and use it as a starting point to discuss and build clarity about the work you, your staff, and other colleagues will do together.

3. Share the collaboration pyramid with department chairs, area leaders, or other staff in leadership positions. Lead a discussion about the collaboration occurring in your school. How might current activities be moved to increasingly higher levels of the pyramid? What effect might such changes have on efforts to redesign and refocus learning and teaching practices?

4. Identify colleagues (in and outside your school) who might also be interested in embarking on the innovation journey. Initiate a conversation and share your learning about the promises of personalized learning and the need to redesign the learning environment in schools.

Appendix A:
An Action Plan for Implementation

Redesigning the learning ecosystem is not a matter of following a set recipe. The process requires leadership, courage, and vision. It draws on a set of principles and it follows a pattern, but it also invites us to integrate fundamental beliefs and understanding about motivation, learning processes, and the purposes of building knowledge and skills in formal education.

Personalized learning places a core priority on developing students' capacity to learn and positions students at the center of the ecosystem as active agents in their own learning. To build learning capacities, teachers work with students to set goals, plan lessons, monitor progress, and demonstrate proficiency. They also help students to develop a sense of purpose and efficacy, build internal motivation and ownership for their own learning, and ultimately become less dependent on external structures and support to drive their learning paths.

As we have worked with our network of schools and districts, we have borrowed from the work and writings of innovation consultant and theorist John Kotter, who has outlined a clear and accessible process for stimulating, initiating, stabilizing, and scaling innovation (2007). We have applied a modified version of Kotter's process successfully to the challenge of building an ecosystem to support personalized learning. Regardless of your experience with change processes and personalized learning, Kotter's sequence of actions can provide useful guidance to your efforts. We share them here along with sample actions you can take to move the personalization process forward.

1. Build Awareness

- Share stories and data from your school demonstrating that the outmoded industrial model of education (see p. 22) may not be preparing all learners for successful futures. Beyond test scores, dropout information, and attendance, consider levels of student engagement (including those of seemingly high-performing students who are "just doing school") and discipline data that may suggest students aren't finding value and purpose in their learning.
- Reflect on and share observations showing that despite everyone's best efforts and a large investment of financial resources, academic results are still not where they need to be for all learners.
- Focus your attention and discussions on the need for a better approach, not on blaming people. Remember: when people are blamed for failures of a system, the problem is almost never the people—it is the system.
- Identify and share resources on personalized learning, especially those that focus on changing the role of students to be more active agents in their learning experience.
- Look for examples of successful personalized learning in practice, preferably locally.

2. Construct New Mental Models

- Share the examples of assumptions about how schools are designed and operated discussed in Chapter 1 (see p. 19) and invite staff and possibly other stakeholders to consider how schools and learning might be different if you replaced these assumptions with ones that reflect what is known about students, learning, and what really works.

- Use the resources and examples you and members of your staff have collected, shared, and studied to begin building an alternative picture of how you can engage students in the process of learning.
- Initiate an ongoing analysis and discussion of the logic and honeycomb models discussed in Chapters 1 and 2 and how they might inform your thinking about students, learning, and instruction.
- Be sure to keep the focus on changing the role of students and the work of learning, and avoid allowing structures such as grade configurations, classroom organization, and student grouping, schedules, and class assignments, grading processes, or technology to become distractors at this point in the process.
- Develop a list of ways in which this approach to learning and teaching will be different from what you have in place today. Include why and how each change will serve to support the learning experience you want for every student. Identify the practices and assumptions you will leave behind because they are holding back the work you need to do.

3. Create a Compelling Shared Vision

- Develop a picture—using words, graphics, or other symbols—of how students will be engaged and supported and how instructional processes will be organized when the redesign is complete and implemented. Revise as needed.
- Be sure to keep the focus of the vision on how the experiences of students will change in ways that will create a path to success for all.

- Coach educators to remain focused on the benefits for student learning rather than on implications for adults. There will be time to figure the latter out later.
- Avoid allowing the vision to become too tightly tied to you or your team. The process of innovation requires shared ownership and commitment. If others are not expressing and demonstrating commitment to the vision at this point, you probably need to retrace your actions and reengage people in the process.
- Share the reasons why you see the vision you and others have created as compelling and worth pursuing, and ask others to share their perspectives. Listen carefully to what you hear, thoughtfully address concerns, and repeat those reasons you know to be important and worth pursuing.

4. Identify Entry Points

- Focus early attention on the three core components: learner profiles, proficiency-based progress, and customized learning paths. These elements will serve as the platform for subsequent entry points as you build your personalized learning model.
- Consider where existing instructional practices and skills are aligned to the model you are creating. Leverage these elements as entry points.
- Identify a small to moderately sized group of staff to launch the innovation process. Look particularly for staff members who are highly interested in the work, are willing to take reasonable risks, and already understand and are oriented toward practices associated with student-centered learning. This group can lead your school and pave the way for future expansion as experience and readiness grow.
- Be clear and transparent about the scope and focus of the early work. There is no benefit to overpromising or overreaching at this point.

- Commit to providing cover, support, and key resources to the initial group of "scouts." You need to create a high potential for success, but you also must keep an eye on how innovation will be scaled and be built out over time.

5. Find Quick Wins

- Spend time visiting with learners and educators, asking them about their experiences and reflections. Listen for learning and victories that embody your vision. Reinforce and share what you hear.
- Watch for shifts in thinking and behavior that align to the changes you are advocating and leading. Recognize and share widely what you see and hear.
- Share stories you hear about students experiencing increased levels of choice, voice, and ownership in their learning.
- Pass along comments from educators about the excitement, renewal, and impact they are having with the new model.
- Watch for leading indicators such as reduced office referrals for misbehavior, increased completion of learning goals, and improved attendance, all of which predict improvements in lagging indicators such as test scores, grades, and graduation rates.

6. Consolidate Examples of Transformation

- Build on quick wins by focusing on the processes and practices that represent the vision of personalized learning, are consistent with the core elements of the model, and are generating early success.
- Collect and share emerging data around leading indicators that show changes are making a difference in the experiences of students and shifting their relationship to learning.

- Support those engaged in the work of transformation as they share what they are learning and urge everyone to listen to, learn from, and apply the positive elements emerging from the new approach.
- Seek out and collect the reactions and perceptions of students as their experience with personalized learning grows. Student voices can be powerful incentives for recruiting more staff to take up the work of innovation and countering critics who may be more comfortable with the traditional, industrial approach to schooling.
- Compare emerging processes and practices to current research on motivation, efficacy and persistence building, purpose, and autonomy as powerful drivers of learning and share them with stakeholders.
- Move others beyond the perception that only a few talented and committed staff members can participate successfully in the new ecosystem. Make the work accessible to anyone who is willing to make the shift in thinking, build practice in the new model, and trust the implementation process.

7. Move Models Toward Scale

- Maintain an invitational approach to staff whose interest in and commitment to the transformation are growing. At this point, your goal is to build confidence that the new approach can work. You do not need to create premature fear and resistance before the local evidence of effectiveness in your setting is strong enough to withstand assault.
- Provide ample opportunities for all staff to observe, reflect on, and adapt their practice in the direction of the new model. Encourage reflection and dialogue among students and staff engaged in personalized learning to build credibility, enthusiasm, and confidence that the new approach is one everyone can and needs to adopt.

- As soon as is practical, launch a second cohort of educators—"pioneers"—to build on the experience of the scouts who launched first. Share everything you and others have learned from initial implementation experiences to support the second and subsequent groups of innovators.
- Keep the focus on student learning and continue to guard against having space, furniture, technology, schedules, and other structural elements become distractions. However, keep in mind that structural elements will need more attention as you scale to avoid having them become barriers to the work. Look for opportunities to make adjustments in these areas if they can accelerate progress. At this point, you and your staff will be in a much better position to decide what needs to be done and will be better able to avoid making changes and purchases that are not aligned to personalized learning.
- Be prepared for occasional "plateauing" and even some slippage in the work of implementation. These are times to reinforce the vision and remind everyone of why the work is important and what it will take to tap the full potential that personalized learning can offer.

8. Institutionalize Practices and Structures

- As more and more staff members become engaged in new practices and are comfortable with students being more active agents in their own learning, you will need to shift your language from talking about personalized learning as an innovation and increasingly describe it as the way learning is nurtured and supported in your school.
- Constantly press the question: How can we make personalized learning available to more learners, and how can we continue to improve the experience?
- Take regular inventory of the policies, structures, and processes utilized throughout the school to ensure that they

are aligned to the work of personalization. These elements, which early on could have been considered distractions, are key now to supporting practice, sustaining momentum, accelerating progress, and stabilizing the system.

- Watch for a tendency among some to press for compromise with "good practices" in the legacy model of education while still using the language of innovation. Return to the vision and reinforce the reasons and reality driving the transformation. Understand that fear may lie behind such calls, in which case reassurance and support, skill building, and additional professional learning may be needed. Don't assume that reluctance among staff is driven by a lack of interest, laziness, or an unwillingness to change. Stay focused on the reasons why personalization is important, and listen and respond to reluctant staff members' concerns.

- Continue to collect, analyze, and share leading indicators of progress and learning success under the new model. Be patient and accept that traditional indicators of effectiveness such as increases in test scores, acceleration in learning, and increased student risk taking will take some time to emerge. As they do, capture, analyze, and share the data to continue building and reinforcing a commitment to improving the work of personalization.

Appendix B:
Sample Design Principles

A number of schools and districts in our action network have found value in creating a set of design principles to function as guides for and checks on their work. By establishing design principles that are consistent with a vision of personalized learning, staff members, design teams, parents, and community members will have a clear description of the purpose and parameters of the work and how learners will experience learning in the new ecosystem. Consider using the following sample set of design principles to support your work.

Student experiences and incentives are designed to build commitment rather than compliance. We know that students who are committed to their learning focus on what is useful to their futures rather than what is expected or demanded of them at the moment.

Pace of learning and level of challenge are calibrated so that success remains within reach while still requiring effort. When educators present learning at a manageable pace, students are more likely to persist and progress in their learning.

Learning, rather than instruction, is the focus. Traditional education environments were designed to place the teacher and instruction at the center of action and attention. If we hope to engage, develop, and position all learners for success, then learning must be the focus. To state the obvious: if learning does not occur, it does not matter how skilled the teacher or respected the instructional practice.

Instructional strategies are designed to foster learning independence. In a world where change is rapid, constant, and unpredictable, we do learners a disservice by limiting them to evaluating their work solely on learning paths prescribed by others and to monitoring how well they follow directions. Instead, educators need to employ instructional strategies that encourage students to build their own paths.

Students are encouraged and expected to own their learning. In traditional settings, students typically are provided with limited (if any) choice or voice in what and how they will learn.As a result, students have little reason to feel strong committment to or ownership of their work. Yet when students *do* understand that learning is an investment and that the results of it are proprietary to them, the likelihood that they will take ownership of it skyrockets.

Student learning capacity is seen as malleable and something that can be developed through practice. Baked into the design of traditional schools was the assumption that some people are born with academic talent and the capacity to learn and others are not. Yet today we know that learning skills can be taught, practiced, and developed. Just because initial attempts don't yield success doesn't prove that success is not possible or that learning capacity cannot be increased. In a world where the definition of what it means to be smart is constantly changing, we need schools to build learning capacity, not just document it.

Learning, not time, is positioned as the constant. Traditional learning ecosystems were designed to have whole cohorts of students progress through the curriculum at a predetermined pace regardless of whether some either required more time or were capable of moving at a quicker pace. By contrast, a personalized learning environment measures progress based on each student's optimal pace of learning. Consequently, some learners take more time while others take less. In the end, learning will be the key measure, not the calendar or schedule

Learning success is designed and built into the learning path. This principle rejects the assumption that learning success is not practical or possible for many students. Rather, it focuses attention on high-quality, well-matched learning challenges and instructional support from the beginning. As a result, the "failure" experienced by so many students is avoided, and when struggles do occur, adjustments and assistance are available to encourage and support students to persist and succeed.

Students see value and purpose in their learning, so they engage and persist in it. Historically, we have not focused enough on helping students to see the purpose of what they are asked to learn. This principle asks us to be clear about the purpose of what we ask students to learn and to involve students in this understanding, even inviting them to help to define the purpose and make personal connections to it.

Appendix C:
Personalized Learning Skill
Sets for Educators

1. **Constructivism.** The teacher understands constructivist learning theory.
2. **Personalized Learning Tools.** The teacher designs and uses personalized learning tools to guide students as architects of their own learning.
3. **Voice and Choice.** The teacher engages students as educational decision-makers by allowing them a degree of voice and choice in their learning.
4. **Learner Independence.** The teacher guides learners to independent mastery of material.
5. **Standards and Learning Progressions.** The teacher understands standards and learning progressions and uses them to support learning.
6. **Assessment.** The teacher creates and uses assessments as, of, and for learning.
7. **Environment.** The teacher uses a variety of learning environments to maximize the potential for student success.

8. **Content Curation.** The teacher curates content, connecting learners to multiple sources and tools.
9. **College and Career Readiness.** The teacher accelerates the college and career readiness of all learners.
10. **Collaboration and Partnerships.** The teacher creates partnerships with parents, community members, content experts, and others outside the school to support learning.

Bibliography

Ames, C. (1992). Classrooms: Goals, structures, and student motivation. *Journal of Educational Psychology, 84*(3), 261–271.

Bandura, A. (1986). *Social foundations of thought and action: A social cognitive theory.* Englewood Cliffs, NJ: Prentice Hall.

Bandura, A. (1991, February). Human agency: The rhetoric and the reality. *American Psychologist, 46*(2), 157–162.

Black, P., & Wiliam, D. (1998). Assessment and classroom learning. *Assessment in Education: Principles, Policy and Practice, 5*(1), 7–73.

Bloom, B. (1984, June/July). The 2 sigma problem: The search for methods of group instruction as effective as one-to-one tutoring. *Educational Researcher, 13*(6), 4–16.

Brandt, R. (1992, December/January). On outcome-based education: A conversation with Bill Spady. *Educational Leadership, 50*(4), 66–70.

Bramante, F., & Colby, R. (2012). *Off the clock: Moving education from time to competency.* Thousand Oaks, CA: Corwin.

Brewster, C., & Fager, J. (2000, October). *Increasing student engagement and motivation: From time-on-task to homework.* Portland, OR: Northwest Regional Educational Laboratory.

Bryk, A., Gomez, L., Grunow, A., & Lemahieu, P. (2015, January/February). Breaking the cycle of failed school reforms. *Harvard Education Letter.*

Center for Research on Educational Outcomes. (2009). *Multiple choice: Charter school performance in 16 states.* Stanford, CA: Stanford University.

CESA #1 (2010). *Transforming public education: A regional call to action.* Pewaukee, WI: Author.

Corbett, D., & Wilson, B. (1995). Make a difference with, not for, students: A plea to researchers and reformers. *Educational Researcher, 24*(5), 12–17.

Darling-Hammond, L., Chung Wel, R., Andree, R., Richardson, N., & Orphanos, S. (2009). *Professional learning in the learning profession: A status report on teacher development in the United States and abroad.* Stanford, CA: National Staff Development Council and the School Redesign Network at Stanford University.

Duckworth, A., Peterson, C., Matthew, M., & Kelly, D. (2007). Grit: Perseverance and passion for long-term goals. *Journal of Personality and Social Psychology, 92*(6), 1087–1101.

Dweck, C. S. (2000). *Self-theories: Their role in motivation, personality, and development.* Philadelphia: Psychology Press.

Dweck, C. S. (2006). *Mindset: The new psychology of success.* New York: Random House.

Fischer-Tubbs, T. (2015, June 5). Personal communication.

Fletcher, A. (2008, November). The Architecture of Ownership. *Educational Leadership, 66*(3).

Frontier, T., & Rickabaugh, J. (2014). *Five levers to improve learning: How to prioritize for powerful results in your schools.* Alexandria, VA: ASCD.

Fullan, M. (2011). *Choosing the wrong drivers for whole school reform.* Victoria, British Columbia: Centre for Strategic Education.

Gallup. (2013). *Fourth annual Gallup student poll.* Washington, DC: Author.

Graves, J. (2010, May). The academic impact of multi-track year-around school calendars: A response to school overcrowding. *Journal of Urban Economics, 67*(3), 378–391.

Greenstone, G. (2010, January/February). The history of bloodletting. *British Columbia Medical Journal, 52*(1).

Hall, T. E., Meyer, A., & Rose, D. H. (2012). *Universal design for learning in the classroom: Practical applications.* Guilford Press.

Hanover Research. (2015). *Program evaluation—personalized learning—next generation learning.* Arlington, VA: Author.

Hattie, J. (2009). *Visible learning: A synthesis of over 800 meta-analyses relating to achievement.* London: Routledge.

Hattie, J. (2012). *Visible learning for teachers: Maximizing impact on learning.* London: Routledge.

Illeris, K. (2004). *Three dimensions of learning: Contemporary learning theory in the tension field between the cognitive, the emotional and the social.* Malabar, FL: Krieger.

Jensen, E. & Nickelsen, L. (2008). *Deeper learning: 7 powerful strategies for in-depth and longer-lasting learning.* Thousand Oaks, CA: Corwin.

Kay, K., & Greenhill, V. (2012). *The leader's guide to 21st century education.* Upper Saddle River, NJ: Pearson.

Keller, J. (2000, February). *How to integrate learner motivation planning into lesson planning: The ARCS model approach.* Paper presented at VII Seminario, Santiago, Cuba. Available: http://mailer.fsu.edu/~jkeller/Articles/Keller%202000%20ARCS%20Lesson%20Planning.pdf

Kohn, A. (1993, September). Choices for children: Why and how to let students decide. *Phi Delta Kappan.* Available: http://www.alfiekohn.org/teaching/cfc.htm

Kohn, A. (2010). How to create nonreaders: Reflections on motivation, learning, and sharing power. *English Journal, 100*(1).

Kotter, J. (2007, January). Leading change: Why transformation efforts fail. *Harvard Business Review.*

Loveless, T. (2012). *How well are American students learning?* Washington, DC: Brookings Institution.

Lumsden, L. S. (1994). *Student motivation to learn.* Eugene, OR: ERIC Clearinghouse on Educational Management.

Marzano, R. (2000, May). Instructional coherence: Changing the role of the teacher. *Educational Leadership, 56*(8), 16–21.

Marzano, R. J. (2007). *The art and science of teaching: A comprehensive framework for effective instruction.* Alexandria, VA: ASCD.

Mitra, D. (2008). Amplifying student voice. *Educational Leadership, 66*(3), 20–25.

Mynard, J., & Sorflaten, R. (2002). *Independent learning in your classroom.* Paper presented at the TESOL Arabia 2002 conference.

National Commission on Excellence in Education. (1983). *A nation at risk: The imperative for educational reform.* Washington, DC: Author.

North Central Regional Educational Laboratory. (1995). *Critical issue: Working toward student self-direction and personal efficacy as educational goals.* Available: http://www.ncrel.org/sdrs/areas/issues/students/learning/lr200.htm

Northwest Evaluation Association. (2014). *Using MAP data to support a personalized learning model.* Available: https://www.nwea.org/page/3/?s=Case+Studies/resources/west-allis-west-milwaukee-school-district/

Ontario Ministry of Education. (2010). *Growing success: Assessment, evaluation and reporting in Ontario schools.* Toronto, Ontario: Author.

Osberg, K. M. (1997). *Constructivism in practice: The case for meaning-making in the virtual world.* Unpublished doctoral dissertation. Seattle: University of Washington.

Pahlke, E., Hyde, J. S. & Allison, C. M. (2014). The effects of single-sex compared with coeducational schooling on students' performance and attitudes: A meta-analysis. *Psychological Bulletin: American Psychological Association, 140*(4), 1042–1072.

Payne, C. M. (2008). *So much reform, so little change: The persistence of failure in urban schools.* Cambridge, MA: Harvard Education Press.

Petty, G. (2009). *Teaching today: A practical guide* (4th ed.). Cheltenham, UK: Nelson Thornes.

Pewaukee School District. (2015). *Pewaukee School District data report.* Pewaukee, WI: Author.

Pink, D. H. (2009). *Drive: The surprising truth about what motivates us.* New York: Riverhead Books.

Radcliffe, D. (2008). A pedagogy-space technology (PST) framework for designing and evaluating learning spaces. *Next Generation Learning Spaces,* 11–16.

Rajagopal, K. (2011). *Create success: Unlocking the potential of urban students.* Alexandria, VA: ASCD.

Ravitch, D. (2010) *The death and life of the great American school system: How testing and choice are undermining education.* New York: Basic Books.

Roemer, M. (2015, February 16). Personal communication.

Schlechty, P.C. (2011). *Engaging students: The next level of working on the work.* San Francisco: Jossey-Bass.

Schmoker, M., & Marzano, R. (1999, March). Realizing the promise of standards-based education. *Educational Leadership, 56*(17–21).

Schunk, D. (1991). Self-efficacy and academic motivation. *Educational Psychologist, 26*(3/4), 207–231.

Sinatra, G. (2000, April). *From passive to active to intentional: Changing conceptions of the learner.* Paper presented at the American Educational Research Association, New Orleans, Louisiana.

Spady, W., & Marshall, K. (1991). Beyond traditional outcome-based education. *Educational Leadership, 49,* 67–72.

Springer, M. G., Ballou, D., Hamilton, L., Le, V., Lockwood, J. R., McCaffrey, D., Pepper, M., & Stecher, B. M. (2012). *Final report: experimental evidence from the project on incentives in teaching (POINT).* Nashville, TN: National Center on Performance Incentives, Vanderbilt University Peabody College.

State of Victoria, Department of Education and Training. (2009). *Making the most of flexible learning spaces.* (2011, January). Melbourne, Australia: Author.

Stefanou, C. R., Perencevich, K. C., DiCintio, M., & Turner, J. C. (2004). Supporting autonomy in the classroom: Ways teachers encourage student decision making and ownership. *Educational Psychologist, 39*(2), 97–110.

Tamim, R. M., Bernard, R. M., Barokhovski, E., Abrami, P. C., & Schmid, R. F. (2011, March). What forty years of research says about the impact of technology on learning: A second order meta-analysis and validation study. *Review of Educational Research, 81*(1), 4–28.

U.S. Department of Education. (2010). *National education technology plan.* Washington, DC: Author.

Wenger, E., McDermott, R., & Snyder, W. (2002). *Cultivating communities of practice: A guide to managing knowledge.* Cambridge, MA: Harvard Business School.

Williams, M., Moyer, J., & Jenkins, S. (2014). *District conditions for scale: A practical guide to scaling personalized learning.* New York: KnowledgeWorks.

Wilson, S., & Peterson, P. (2006, July). *Theories of learning and teaching: What do they mean for educators?* Washington, DC: National Education Association.

Witte, J. R., Carlson, D., Cowen, J. M., Fleming, D. J., & Wolf, P. J. (2011). *MPCP longitudinal educational growth study: Fourth-year report.* Fayetteville: University of Arkansas.

Wolf, M. A. (2010). *Innovate to educate: System redesign for personalized learning.* Washington, DC: Software and Information Industry Association.

Worthy, J. (2010). Only the names have been changed: Ability grouping revisited. *Urban Review, 42*(5), 271–295.

Zepeda, S., & Mayers, R. (2006). An analysis of research on block scheduling. *Review of Educational Research, 76*(1), 278–391.

Zimmerman, B. J., Bandura, A., & Martinez-Pons, M. (1992). Self-motivation for academic attainment: The role of self-efficacy beliefs and personal goal setting. *American Educational Research Journal, 29*(3), 663–676.

Index

Note: Page numbers followed by an italicized *f* indicate information contained in figures.

About the Author

James Rickabaugh is the director of the Institute for Personalized Learning, an education innovation lab dedicated to transforming public education. The institute serves a growing number of member school districts engaged in personalized learning and is a part of the multistate Innovation Lab Network coordinated by the Council of Chief State School Officers.

James formerly served as superintendent of the Whitefish Bay School District in Southeastern Wisconsin and other districts in Wisconsin and Minnesota. He was named "Wisconsin Superintendent of the Year" in 2008 and "Minnesota Superintendent of the Year" in 1996. He received the Excellence in Educational Leadership award in 2005 from the University Council for Educational Administration and a lifetime achievement award from the Master Teachers in 2010. James is an engaging speaker and has presented on personalized learning at several national and international conferences. He also provides retreat and meeting facilitation and consultation for school boards, leadership teams, and professional staffs. He can be reached by e-mail at jrickabaugh@cesa1.k12.wi.us or on Twitter at @drrickabaugh.